Bible Fun St...

D1647921

FOR AGES 7-9

ROCK the Room Games

David C Cook®

transforming lives together

ROCK THE ROOM GAMES
Published by David C. Cook
4050 Lee Vance View
Colorado Springs, CO 80918 U.S.A.

David C. Cook Distribution Canada
55 Woodslee Avenue, Paris, Ontario, Canada N3L 3E5

David C. Cook U.K., Kingsway Communications
Eastbourne, East Sussex BN23 6NT, England

David C. Cook and the graphic circle C logo
are registered trademarks of Cook Communications Ministries.

Written by Jodi Hoch, Renee Gray-Wilburn
Cover Design by BMB Design/ Scott Johnson
Interior Design by TrueBlue Design/Sandy Flewelling
Illustrations by Robbie Short, William D. Schultz, Sarah Nocholl | Dreamstime.com, Sandy Flewelling

Scripture quotations, unless otherwise noted, are taken from the
HOLY BIBLE, NEW INTERNATIONAL VERSION®. Copyright © 1973,
1978, 1984 by International Bible Society. Used by permission of
Zondervan. All rights reserved.

ISBN 978-1-4347-6718-9

First Printing 2009
Printed in the United States

1 2 3 4 5 6 7 8 9 10

David C Cook®
transforming lives together

TABLE OF Contents

HOW TO Rock Your Room

Rock the Room Games is a fun-filled, activity-based resource designed to lead your 7- to 9-year-olds through an adventure in God's Word. *Rock the Room Games* presents page after page of spirited games that incorporate team building, sharing, and problem-solving concepts. The children will love the excitement and entertainment offered with each game. And best of all, they'll learn biblical principles and God's Word with each and every activity.

Each game includes the following to help you make the most of each activity:

Bible Background—nuggets of information regarding the Bible story

Teacher Tips—optional playing ideas and suggestions on ramping up the challenge, as well as easier ways to play

Level/Group Size/Space Required—brief description of the energy level required for play, along with how many players and how much space you'll need

Warm Up—how to set up playing area and prepare materials ahead of time

Stuff You Need—supplies needed to play the game

Action!—actual game instructions with suggested script to help you engage players

Link It Up—thought-provoking questions that tie the game's application to the Bible reference and everyday life.

To effectively use your game time, keep the game explanation brief, and prepare yourself by knowing how the game relates to the Bible reference. Allow adequate time for your games, but don't overplay them—stop while everyone's still having fun! Most importantly, have fun yourself. Your attitude and spirit while leading the games will be contagious to everyone involved.

The 26 activities in this book can be done in any order and easily fit into any curriculum. Simply use the Scripture and Topic Index on page 110 to match a game with the lesson you're teaching. These activities also can be used as alternate Step Three activities in several curriculum lines: David C. Cook Bible-In-Life, Echoes, LifeLINKS to God, College Press, Reformation Press, Wesley, Anglican, and The Cross. If you have one of these lines, look through the Correlation Chart on page 111 and find the activity geared to your lesson. You'll use this new activity instead of one of the other Step Three activities listed in your teacher's guide. This book, when combined with *Fun and Freaky Science,* will give you a full year's worth of Step Three replacement activities for the elementary age group.

Creation Scramble

A wild race to unscramble the days of Creation!

Bible Basis:
Genesis 1:6–13, 28–29

Memory Verse:
God saw all that he had made, and it was very good. Genesis 1:31a

BIBLE background

On the second day of Creation, God separated the waters so there was water above the sky and water under the sky. While this does not resemble what we see in the earth today, it could be that God placed a layer of water vapor around the earth, very high up in the atmosphere. This would have created a greenhouse effect, enabling plants to flourish. Some believe this could also be why people lived so long in the "early days" and why so much water came from the sky during the Flood (Gen. 7:11).

On the third day, God created all the vegetation on earth. By supplying all the plants that would produce fruit and seeds, He was not only providing for the perpetuity of plant life here on earth, He was also setting up the perfect environment for animal and human life.

Even though we may not totally understand all the ways God created as He did, the fact remains that when He spoke, it happened. God said that everything He made was very good. "Everything" also includes you. Never doubt that you are part of God's perfect plan for this earth and that He has a very special job for you to do. Ask Him to show you His plans for your life, including how He desires to use you in teaching the children in your class today.

TEACHER tips

✱ If playing in a large space and with two teams, add a tag element to the game, so that players from opposing teams must tag each other. Players who are tagged then drop the card they're carrying right where they're tagged and return to their team's starting point before continuing play.

✱ If you do add a tag element, discuss and demonstrate what a "proper" tag looks and feels like so that no one is hurt. Praise those players who properly tag others during the game.

✱ As the game is being played, shout out commands (hop on one foot, crawl on all fours, crab walk, etc.). Players continue play while following actions until a new action is given.

WARM up

1. On one side of 6 index cards draw a simple figure from each day of Creation (sun, cloud, tree, fish, animal, man). Optional: Copy the figures supplied on page 9 and glue onto index cards. Repeat so that you have 10 sets of cards, for 60 cards total. If playing with 2 teams, make 2 sets of cards of each figure using a different color index card for each team.

2. Mark out creation zones using masking tape.

3. Spread cards face up in playing area, avoiding creation zones.

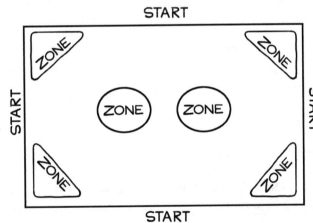

STUFF you need

◎ Masking tape

◎ 60 index cards

◎ Markers

◎ Optional: glue and scissors

ACTion!

Players begin by standing around outside edge of playing area or in a designated starting area.

God created our amazing world in six days. He was very busy! Your job is to get busy as a team and collect cards to put into the different creation zones that match the different days of creation. There are 10 sets of six different cards. Each card has a picture of one thing God created on each of the different days.

Run into the playing area and pick up a card—but only one card at a time! Put that card in one of the six creation zones, depending on what picture is on it.

Creation zones will only have one type of card in them (all suns, all trees, etc.). Don't tell players which zones are which. They'll need to work as a team to figure that out.

After all 60 cards have been placed in the correct creation zones the game is over. What did God do on the seventh day of Creation? Allow for answers. Yes! He rested! When you've finished the game, everyone lie down and rest.

* **Large group option:** The whole group works together. Time them to see how quickly they can work together to complete the challenge.

* **Team play option:** Each team chooses a color represented by the card colors. Teams begin play at the same time. The first team to correctly place all their cards into the creation zones wins.

LINK it up

God created the entire world in only six days, and then He rested. God is very organized and knows just what to do and when to do it. He planned it so our world would be perfect.

* You probably didn't feel very organized while playing our game today. Some jobs require a lot of order and organization—like creating the universe! What are some things you have a hard time being organized about? (*doing homework, cleaning my room, doing chores, etc.*)

* Even God worked as a team with Jesus and the Holy Spirit when He made our world. What was the hardest part about playing as a team today? (*Answers may vary.*)

* God created a useful and beautiful world. Why do you think He made it not only useful, but beautiful as well? (*Answers may vary.*)

Body Building

Which team can be first to build a body in God's image ... with bags?

Bible Basis:

Genesis 1:26—2:25; 3:8

Memory Verse:

God created man in his own image, in the image of God he created him; male and female he created them. Genesis 1:27

BIBLE background

God created us in His likeness. Stop and think about that for a minute. What does it mean for us to be like Him? We know from Scripture that we have His spiritual characteristics and that we are able to make moral choices. We also have sovereignty over the earth, which comes with responsibility to care for the earth He has given us.

When sin entered the world through Adam, the image of God in humans was defaced. But we all still bear God's image to some degree. As believers become more Christlike, that image of God is being restored in them (2 Cor. 3:18). However, Christ is the only one who bears the image of God perfectly (Heb. 1:3).

As spiritual beings, unlike any other creature He made, we are able to relate to God spirit to spirit. When we die, our spirits will live eternally. John 3:16 promises that those who believe in Jesus will have everlasting life with Him.

When you consider the great care and love God put into making His most prized creation, there should be no place for low self-image or poor self-esteem. Think about it—God made you to be just like Him! It doesn't get any better than that! Help your class begin to realize the depth of God's love for them, enabling their self-worth to be tied solely to the value He places on them.

level:
Moderate

group size:
Enough for two to four teams

space required:
Classroom or gym

TEACHER tips

✼ For added challenge, have all team members number off. Players can only retrieve bags when their number is called.

✼ Adding eyes, a mouth, ears, arms, etc., to the number of bags needed to complete a person will also increase the challenge.

✼ For easier play, make each paper bag person in the same color for each team (seven bags with all red markers, seven bags with all blue markers, etc.).

WARM up

1. Draw 7 different body part figures on 7 paper grocery bags, forming a complete person: head, heart, left hand, right hand, torso, left leg with foot, and right leg with foot. Create a complete set of 7 bags per team, plus a few extra parts.

2. Use masking tape or other boundary marker to designate the playing area. Create four squares in the corners of the playing area with the tape, as well as a large circle in the center.

3. Lay bags facedown in the center circle of the playing area and shuffle.

STUFF you need

◎ Masking tape

◎ Markers

◎ Large brown grocery bags with 1 non-printed side

ACTion!

Demonstrate what a completed person made of the bags looks like.

The Bible tells us that God made us in His image. Point to the bag person parts while discussing each one. **He gave us each a head with a mind to think like He does. He gave us each a torso that contains everything to keep our bodies running perfectly. He gave us a heart that we should fill with love for Him and those around us. He also gave us hands and feet to help others and to do His work on the earth.**

God put Adam, the first man, together in an instant by forming him from the dust of the ground and then breathing life into him. Let's play a game to see how fast you can put a person together. The first team to form a complete person wins!

Begin the game with players standing as a team in their squares (see playing area sketch on page 13). To start play, one player from each team runs to the center of the playing area and picks up two bags. The players open the bags, put them on their feet, and run back to their squares. Each team then removes the bags from their player's feet, folds the bags flat, and begins to build their body by laying the bags on the floor. As soon as the bags are off the player's feet, the next player in line can either run to the center for two more bags or return one or two bags of unnecessary parts. If bags are returned, new bags cannot be retrieved on the same turn. The team must wait until that player returns to the square before sending a new player for more bags.

Teams may never have more than eight bags in their squares at one time. Players may retrieve or return one or two bags at a time. Bags must be worn on the players' feet whenever transporting bags.

LINK it up

God made you to be just like Him. There is no other creature on earth as amazing as you. You can think, feel, move, and best of all, talk to God. You are a wonderful creation!

* **What are some ways you can show God you appreciate your body and the perfect way He made you?** *(caring for it by eating good foods, getting exercise, being happy with the way He made me, etc.)*

* **What are some ways you can use your body to worship God?** *(dance, sing, pray, help others, etc.)*

✱ Even though God made us all to be like Him, He also made each of us
very different from one another. Name some ways you are different
from the person sitting next to you. *(Answers will vary and may include
physical differences as well as personality differences. Encourage positive
answers that emphasize the fact that those differences were granted by God,
who loves variety and made each of us to be unique and special.)*

Stomping Out Sin

Players pop as many balloons as possible as they stomp out sin.

Bible Basis:

Genesis 4:1–16

Memory Verse:

The Lord is a God who knows, and by him deeds are weighed.
1 Samuel 2:3

BIBLE background

Genesis doesn't directly give a reason why God accepted Abel's offering from the flock but rejected Cain's offering of grain. Some believe that Abel's faith and attitude were better than Cain's, whose heart was later revealed in his fit of rage. Or perhaps it was because Abel had given God "fat portions from some of the firstborn of his flock," while Cain offered God "some of the fruits of the soil," meaning Abel gave God his very best while Cain did not.

Regardless of why Abel's offering was accepted and Cain's was not, Cain became angry with his brother. Not able to contain his jealousy, Cain committed the earth's first murder by ruthlessly killing Abel.

God called out to Cain and asked him, "Where is your brother?" Not realizing that God already knew the answer to His own question, Cain replied, "I don't know." Had Cain admitted his sin right there, forgiveness would have been his. Instead, he tried to hide it from God and refused to repent.

How often do we try to hide our sin from God and run away from Him instead of running to Him when we do something wrong? Forgiveness is always ours for the taking; all we have to do is ask.

level:

Active

group size:

Enough for two to four teams

space required:

Classroom or gym

TEACHER tips

✳ Since this activity involves running and stomping on balloons at the same time, be sure children play safely and watch what they are doing.

✳ As the group of players that has balloons attached gets smaller, try limiting the size of the playing area.

✳ For easier play, run the game as described below but have the balloons lying on the ground, without strings, instead of tying them to the ankles. Players jump or stomp on the other team's balloons, while trying to keep their own balloons from getting stomped on. Team members cannot catch or hold balloons in their hands.

✳ For added challenge, have players play solo rather than on teams. Everyone enters the playing area at the start of the game and players spread out on all sides of the playing area. Each player remains in the playing area until his or her balloon gets popped, at which point that player must leave the game. Give the children one minute for play. In this version, the goal is to pop as many balloons as possible (help your friends get rid of their sin) before time runs out.

STUFF you need

◎ String or heavy yarn

◎ Balloons—
different colors for
different teams (at
least 1 per player)

WARM up

1. Blow up all balloons.

2. Tie a 3-foot piece of yarn or string to the end of each balloon.

ACTion!

Give each player one balloon with attached string. (All the players of a team should have the same color.) Players tie the strings to their right ankles and then stand as teams on opposite ends of playing area.

Cain did a terrible thing by killing his brother, Abel. But what made it worse was that he lied to God and said he didn't know what happened to his brother. God is always ready and willing to forgive us when we do something wrong if we ask Him to.

We can never hide our sin from God. The best thing for us is to not sin to begin with. In today's game, we're going to pretend these balloons are types of sin. Maybe they're sins you're having a hard time beating. When I shout, "Stomp out sin!" run to the opposite side of the playing area. While you're running, try to pop as many balloons as you can to stomp out as much sin as possible.

As players' balloons get popped, they sit out of play. If they get to the other side, they are safe. They'll remain on the opposite side of the playing area until you shout again; then they'll return to the side they began on. Players will continue running back and forth on your command until the last few players remain. Surprise the children: The team with the least players still in the game wins. (They had the most sin stomped out.) If you play a second time, designate the winner as the team who stomps out the most sin (the team with the most balloons left over).

LINK it up

It's never good when we sin. Sin keeps us from having a good relationship with God, and it makes our hearts feel sad. The best thing we can do is to run to God when we sin and ask Him to forgive us. He wants to forgive us more than we know!

✸ **How do you feel when you know you've done something wrong, especially if no one else knows about it?** (*Children's answers may involve feelings of guilt, being sorry, feeling bad, unhappy, or afraid to talk to anyone about it, including talking to God. If you can bring a personal story from your own experience, it may help children put words to their own experiences.*)

✸ **You tried to keep your balloon—which represented sin—from being popped—or removed. Why do you think most people want to try to hide their sin from God, as Cain did?** (*Some people may be afraid that they*

will be punished by God if their sin is found out. Some don't understand that God sees and knows everything and that He wants to forgive us so we can have a close relationship with Him again.) **Compare our relationship with God with similar times when we hurt friends and family and need to ask for forgiveness.**

✱ **What can you do to show God that you're sorry when you sin?** *(tell God that I'm sorry, pray the day's memory verse, try to correct the situation, etc.)*

Rainbow Rescue

Clinging to the rainbow is your only hope for safety when the Flood comes!

Bible Basis:

Genesis 8:1—9:17

Memory Verse:

*Christ Jesus came into the world to save sinners.
1 Timothy 1:15*

BIBLE background

For over a year Noah and his family lived in the ark that he built to escape the Flood. Noah released a dove three times from the ark to test the water level. On the third release, the dove did not return. God had saved Noah and his family, and they safely departed from the ark.

When Noah got off the boat, the first thing he did was build an altar to God to offer burnt sacrifices. God was very pleased with Noah's obedience and instructed Noah and his family to inhabit the land and multiply. God was ready to start His creation afresh.

Because Noah had kept his promise to God, God would now make a promise to Noah. He told Noah and his sons that He would put a rainbow in the sky as a sign of a covenant between Himself and all creatures of the earth. He promised to never again destroy the earth with a flood.

Today, the rainbow is not only a sign of this covenant but also a symbol of God's faithfulness to all His creation. God is a God who keeps His promises to go to the ends of the earth to save His righteous followers.

level:
Moderate to active

group size:
Small to large

space required:
Classroom, gym,
or outdoors

TEACHER tips

✱ If pool noodles are not available, beach towels in rainbow colors may be used. Spread towels on the floor. Players must stand on the towels.

✱ For a more challenging version of the game, choose one or two players to be It, and have them stand in the center of the playing area. Other players must avoid those who are It. If they get tagged, they must sit out of the game.

✱ Use this game to review the Bible story. Ask players a question from the story; then have them run to a pool noodle. Draw a card from the bag. (Return the card to the bag.) Only the players holding that color pool noodle are safe. The other players must sit out. If one of the players who just got out correctly answers the question, all the players are back in the game. Otherwise the players must stay out. Then have all remaining players or the ones who returned to the game run to a different color noodle. Draw a card again. Continue play in this manner.

WARM up

1. Write the color of each pool noodle or towel on 3 index cards.

2. Place cards in a paper bag.

3. Spread out pool noodles in playing area.

STUFF you need

◎ Pool noodles or towels in 4 different colors

◎ 12 index cards

◎ Small brown paper bag

◎ Marker

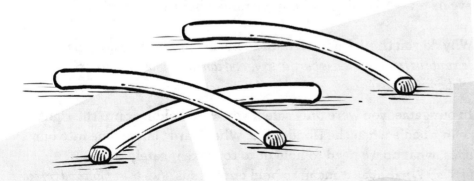

ACTion!

There was a time when God knew He had to get rid of the sin that had taken over the world. He decided to make it start raining and flood the earth to wipe out all of His creation—everyone and everything except Noah, his family, and the animals on the ark. Noah loved God, and God wanted to start His creation over with him.

God had a plan to save Noah, but it meant that Noah would have to follow and obey God for a very long time. When God did save Noah from the Flood, He made Noah a promise that He would never again destroy the earth with a flood. God put a rainbow in the sky as a sign—a reminder of that promise.

We're going to use pool noodles to remind us of God's rainbow. You'll be safe if you're caught holding onto the right color noodle when the flood comes.

Have players begin the game by spreading out and holding onto a pool noodle. When you shout, **"The flood is coming!"** all players run to a different color pool noodle. Draw three cards from the bag, and call out the colors. (Return cards to bag.) The players who are holding onto these colors are safe. The other players must sit out.

Play again, but this time only draw two cards. Continue again, only drawing one card. Play until only one or two players remain.

LINK it up

God got so angry with all the sin that had come into the world, He decided He needed to start all over with creation. He saved Noah and his family because Noah was the only godly man God could find. God is able to save us too—His rainbow helps us remember that.

✱ Why do you think God hates sin so much? (*sin and disobeying God separate us from God, sin is hurtful to us and can cause problems in our lives and relationships, etc.*)

✱ In our game, you were only safe if you were holding onto the right color noodle when the flood came. When hard times come into our lives, what do we need to hold onto to make it safely through? (*Jesus.*) **What does it mean to hold onto Jesus?** (*we trust Him and try our best to follow Him, we stay close to Him and are honest with Him, we tell Him our needs and thank Him for His care, etc.*)

✽ **How can we receive the forgiveness for our sins that God offers?**
(First let the children suggest answers. Bring in the Memory Verse as a simple explanation of salvation. Be ready to give a clear, brief summary of how to receive Christ for those children who are ready for that.)

Get-Along Land

Players learn to get along as they create shapes from their piece of the "land."

Bible Basis:

Genesis 13

Memory Verse:

If it is possible, as far as it depends on you, live at peace with everyone.
Romans 12:18

BIBLE background

Abram, his wife, Sarah, and his nephew Lot left Egypt and went to Bethel. God had made Abram very wealthy, and Lot had many riches as well. Together, their possessions were so great that the land they were on could not support them both. Abram's and Lot's people began fighting among themselves for the land.

Abram quickly put an end to the fighting by telling Lot that he could choose the land he wanted. It was actually Abram's right to choose since he was the elder, but he waived that right to give Lot first choice. Lot chose the fertile plains of the Jordan, which left Abram the mountainous area of Canaan.

Abram solved the dispute in an unselfish manner, which pleased God. Because Abram did not demand his rights, God gave him more than he could have asked for: He promised Abram that all the land he could see would one day belong to his descendants.

One of the hardest things for us to do is to give up our rights and sacrifice for others. Getting along with others is precious in God's sight. When we put others first, God will bless us with more than we could imagine.

level:
Low to moderate

group size:
Small

space required:
Classroom or outdoors

TEACHER tips

* Use more than one tarp for a larger group. Have teams on separate tarps compete against each other.

* For added challenge, add actions while players move the tarp: hold hands, lock elbows, hold up one foot, etc. (see below)

STUFF you need

◎ 9′ to 12′ tarp (can substitute bed sheet, blanket, or shower curtain)

WARM up

Spread out tarp on floor.

ACTion!

Abram, who God later named Abraham, and his nephew Lot traveled together from Egypt and moved into a land that God had prepared for them. They were each so wealthy, the land wasn't big enough to support both of them, their families, and all their possessions.

Abram's and Lot's people began fighting over the land. Abram didn't want to fight, so he told Lot they needed to figure out a way to work together and come up with a plan to decide where they would each live. Abram decided to give up his right to choose the land he wanted and gave Lot first choice of the best land. Abram knew it was important to get along with Lot.

In today's game, your team will need to work together as you figure out ways to do different actions using the tarp, which is your land. Sometimes, like Abram, you may have to give up your rights and the way you'd rather do something and let others have their way.

Have 10 to 12 players stand on the tarp. Announce a challenge—an action to be completed. Players cannot step off the tarp when completing the challenge. Encourage teamwork and cooperation as players complete the challenge. Use the following ideas as actions to complete:

• Move tarp from one place to another (at least 10 feet).

• Fold tarp in half, or as small as possible, with everyone still standing on it.

• Wrap all players in the tarp so no one can be seen (be sure kids leave plenty of open areas for air).

• Form the tarp into shapes from the Bible story (sheep, shepherd's staff, tent, etc.).

LINK it up

Abram knew it was important that he and Lot not fight over the land God gave them. He took the first step and offered Lot the choice of the best land. God blessed Abraham greatly, and one reason is because he gave up his rights for the sake of getting along.

✱ What was the hardest part about having to do all the actions as a team? *(Answers will vary and may focus on issues of communication, cooperation, and leadership.)*

✱ Were there times in the game when you had to give up your rights for the sake of getting along with the team? Explain. *(As children share their*

observations, point out that living in peace with others often requires us to give up our rights in various ways. One good example is that drivers must obey the traffic laws and can't just decide to ignore a red light, or run through a stop sign because they want to move faster. Everyone agrees to follow the traffic laws so that cars won't crash into each other!)

❋ **Think of someone you sometimes have a hard time getting along with. What's one thing you can do to take the first step in trying to get along better with this person?** *(letting the other person take the lead, doing what the other person prefers, being patient with people who have personalities that rub us the wrong way, putting other people first, etc.)*

Tic-Tac-Totally Trust God

Teams learn about trust in this life-size game of tic-tac-toe.

Bible Basis:

Genesis 22:1–19

Memory Verse:

Trust in the Lord forever, for the Lord, the Lord, is the Rock eternal. Isaiah 26:4

BIBLE background

Isaac was Abraham's long-awaited son who was specially promised by God. God had also promised that a nation would be born through this destiny child. Knowing all this, Abraham must have been wondering what God was going to do when He told him to sacrifice Isaac in worship to Him.

If Abraham was shocked, devastated, or frightened by God's command, he didn't show it. Abraham rose up "early the next morning" and prepared his donkey for the journey. He didn't hesitate, and he didn't argue with God. He simply obeyed.

He obviously believed God would do something miraculous—even if that meant raising Isaac from the dead—for he told his servants that he and Isaac would worship and then "we will come back to you." Still, Abraham went as far as tying Isaac to the altar and raising the knife over him. At the very last minute, God stopped him.

Abraham had no idea what God had planned. He only knew to obey and trust the One who had always been faithful. When God tells us what to do through His Word or His voice in our spirit, we immediately have a choice. Will we obey? No, we can't see what lies ahead. No, we have no idea how God will come through. But we can choose to trust the One who is faithful.

level:

Low

group size:

Two small- to
medium-size teams

space required:

Classroom

TEACHER tips

* Generate questions prior to game
(see list that follows), and write
them on index cards. Base the
questions on the Bible story or on
the theme of trusting God. Include
easy questions as well as more
challenging ones.

* For added challenge, tape a circle
around the tic-tac-toe grid. Indicate
two areas on opposite sides where players may enter the circle. Players on
each team sit on the outside of the circle and number off. When you call out a
number, the two players with that number run around the circle clockwise
one time. They then enter the tic-tac-toe grid where indicated and jump on a
square. Ask players sitting outside the circle a question, and have them write
their answers. If correct, their players stay in the grid. Otherwise, players
return to the outside of the circle. Continue until a team achieves a tic-tac-toe.

* For easier play, have players sit around the tic-tac-toe grid. Teams answer
questions, then toss their plate onto the grid. The team with plates in a tic-
tac-toe first wins.

STUFF you need

◎ Masking tape

◎ Markers

◎ Index cards

◎ 12 paper plates

WARM up

1. Mark Xs on 6 paper plates and Os on 6 paper plates.

2. Tape or mark a tic-tac-toe board on the floor as a playing area.

*ACT*ion!

Abraham waited a very long time for his son Isaac to be born. Not only did God promise him this son, but God also promised that He would give birth to a nation through him. So why would God ask Abraham to sacrifice Isaac? Abraham didn't know why, but he chose to obey. He knew God, and he knew he could trust God—even with the life of his son.

We don't always know what God has planned for us, but the more we get to know God, the more we'll realize we can trust Him with our very lives. During this game, you'll need to answer questions about trust in order to jump into the squares and play tic-tac-toe. When a team wins, everyone shout, "Tic-tac-totally trust God!"

Ahead of time, write several game questions on index cards (see the list that follows for ideas). Start with teams sitting on opposite sides of the playing area. Set X plates next to one team and O plates next to the other. Take turns asking each team a question from the index cards. If the team answers the question correctly, they select one player to enter the playing area. Players take a plate and jump directly on a square of their choice. Players must stay in whichever square they chose. Teammates may not help each other determine which square to jump on. Continue asking questions until a team wins.

You may use the following questions, or use them as ideas for generating questions:

- **What did God promise Abraham about his son?** (*A nation would be started through his son.*)
- **How many people traveled to Moriah?** (*Abraham, Isaac, and two servants—a total of four people.*)
- **What did Abraham do before he found the place God told him about?** (*He cut wood for the burnt offering.*)
- **What did Abraham tell the servants that he and Isaac would do?** (*They both would worship and then come back.*)
- **How did Abraham answer when Isaac asked where the sacrifice was?** (*God would provide the lamb.*)
- **Who was going to provide the lamb for the offering?** (*God*)
- **Who stopped Abraham before it was too late?** (*an angel*)
- **What was provided in the bushes?** (*a ram caught by its horns*)
- **How numerous would Abraham's descendants be?** (*as numerous as the stars in the sky and the sand on the seashore*)
- **Why did God bless Abraham?** (*because Abraham was willing to obey Him no matter what.*)

LINK it up

Abraham knew he could trust God with Isaac's life, so he obeyed and took Isaac to be sacrificed. Abraham passed God's test of trust, and the Lord allowed Isaac to live. Sometimes God wants us to prove to Him how much we really trust Him. When we pass the test, our reward will be great.

✱ **What does it mean to be a trustworthy person?** *(you keep your promises, you can be counted on by others, you do your best, etc.)* **Do you think you are a trustworthy person? Why or why not?** *(While most children will be inclined to answer yes, you may want to explore the flipside and discuss what happens when people are not trustworthy.)*

✱ **What was the hardest thing you've had to trust God for?** *(Try to share a story from your own life experience in order to encourage children to think of their own challenges.)*

✱ **Name some people in your life you can trust. Explain why those people have earned your trust.** *(Answers will vary.)*

Race to Forgive

The race is on to tag others with forgiveness.

Bible Basis:
Genesis 27:41—33:17

Memory Verse:
Bear with each other and forgive whatever grievances you may have against one another. Forgive as the Lord forgave you.
Colossians 3:13

BIBLE background

Rebekah discovered that her older son, Esau, wanted to kill his brother, Jacob, because he had cheated Esau. She told Jacob to travel from their home and stay with her brother, Laban. Before Jacob left, his father, Isaac, blessed him and asked God to grant him land and many descendants.

Jacob went to live with his uncle Laban and stayed there 20 years. For seven years he worked for his uncle so that he could marry Laban's daughter, Rachel. But Laban deceived him and gave him his other daughter, Leah, to marry instead. Still, Jacob prospered, as God had promised, and seven years later Jacob married Rachel.

At God's command, Jacob packed up his family and headed back to his homeland. He was very anxious and frightened about seeing Esau again, but he wanted to repent and make things right with his brother. When Esau saw him, he embraced him and forgave him. Jacob was once again accepted by his brother.

What an amazing feeling when we are forgiven by others! It's as if a giant weight has been removed from us. When we hold onto unforgiveness toward someone who has hurt us, we are holding that same weight on them. Ask God to help you forgive those who have wronged you. You have the power to remove the weight and set them—and yourself—free.

level:

Active

group size:

Two teams, any size

space required:

Gym or outdoors

TEACHER tips

* For added challenge, call out a command and point players in opposite directions. There will be confusion until they realize they've been tricked.

* Have players choose a partner, then have partners join hands. Partners must stay together. If one partner gets tagged, the other is also tagged.

* Demonstrate what a "good" tag looks like. Also, discuss what not to do, or where not to go, during the game.

STUFF you need

◎ Masking tape

WARM up

Use masking tape to mark boundaries in playing area.

ACTion!

Divide your group into two teams; then line up the teams in the middle of the playing area. Players should face each other while standing about eight feet apart. At least 20 feet behind each team is their safe zone.

Jacob did a mean thing by pretending to be his brother, Esau, in order to fool their father, Isaac, and receive his blessing—a blessing that was meant for Esau. Jacob cheated his own brother out of his inheritance and made Esau very angry. Jacob left home and lived with his uncle for 20 years. The whole time he had to think about the wrong he had done to his brother.

When Jacob finally came home, he was scared to see Esau again because he thought Esau still hated him. But when Esau saw him, he ran to him, hugged him, and completely forgave him.

In our game, one team is called the Jacobs and the other is the Esaus. Designate which team is which. **You will run as fast as you can to try to tag a person on the other team. If you can reach the your team's safe line without being tagged, you are safe.**

Call out one of two commands: "Jacob forgives Esau" or "Esau forgives Jacob." If you call "Jacob forgives Esau," all of the Jacobs run to tag an Esau before they reach their back line. If the Esuas safely reach the back line, they will return to play again as an Esau. But if they get tagged, they become a Jacob. When they return to the starting lines, they are now in the Jacob's line. Players can only tag one player per round. Players return to center lines to begin again after each round of play.

LINK it up

Jacob did a mean thing to Esau, and he probably thought Esau would never forgive him. But Esau did forgive his brother and accepted him again after all those years.

* **When was a time you forgave somebody for something?** (*Start the sharing by offering a story from your own life.*)

* **Have you been forgiven for doing something wrong? What happened? How did that make you feel?** (*Answers will vary and may touch on feelings of thankfulness, relief, or happiness.*)

* **Why do you think it's so important to God that we forgive others when they hurt us?** (*because He forgave us, because it will make the other person feel better, because it shows God that we love Him, etc.*)

SAFELINE FOR JACOB

JACOB

ESAU

SAFELINE FOR ESAU

✱ In our game, you ran to try to tag the other team with forgiveness. Why is it better that we run to forgive someone instead of waiting a long time?
(God wants us to forgive right away, it's better to make things right quickly rather than wait, forgiving heals hurts, it can be harder to offer forgiveness if we wait too long because our relationship is damaged, etc.)

Unfair Chair Game

Life's not always fair, especially when you're left with no place to sit!

Bible Basis:

Genesis 39:1—41:57

Memory Verse:

I praised the Most High; I honored and glorified him who lives forever.
Daniel 4:34

BIBLE background

Joseph was about 17 when he was sold into slavery and was put into prison soon after that. He was 30 when he was released from jail (Gen. 41:46). In whatever situation Joseph found himself, he did his best. His dependability in prison brought him great favor, and God rewarded him abundantly.

Years earlier, God had given Joseph a dream of his future (Gen. 37:5–11). Although he was unjustly sold into slavery and imprisoned, Joseph chose not to seek retaliation against his brothers or Potiphar's wife. He did nothing whatsoever to promote himself or prove his innocence. Joseph consistently honored God despite several unfair situations he was forced into. As a result of his response to his unfair treatment, as well as his humble attitude, God fulfilled the dream He had given him years earlier, reconciled him to his family, and bestowed great wealth and favor upon him.

We don't know what our individual journeys will hold. God's Word promises us a great future in Him (Jer. 29:11), but that doesn't mean we won't go through some tough times to get there. As we honor God and walk with godly character through our situations, God will be waiting for us with a reward that will make it all worthwhile.

level:
Moderate

group size:
Small to medium

space required:
Classroom or gym

TEACHER tips

✱ Discuss putting safety first by not pushing others to get to a chair. Explain that if there's a tie for a chair, both players go to "jail."

✱ For added challenge, have the players in jail toss small inflatable balls (or foam balls) at the players still walking around the circle. Now they not only have to worry about getting a chair, but also getting hit by balls. This keeps those in jail still involved in the game.

WARM up

1. Place chairs in a circle facing out (as shown below), using one less chair than players.

2. Tie a blindfold over each player's eyes.

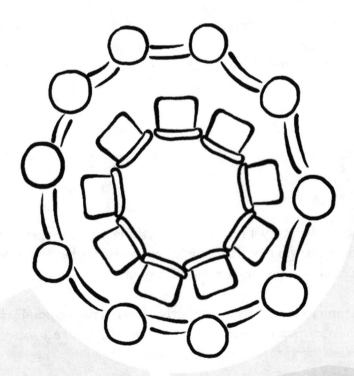

ACTion!

Have blindfolded players stand and form a circle around the chairs. The players should gently place one hand on the shoulder of the child in front of them.

Joseph was a very godly man who had some terrible things happen to him. God had promised him a wonderful future, but his life seemed to be going down the wrong path. Even though he was treated unfairly, like when his brothers beat him and sold him into slavery, and when Potiphar put him in prison for no good reason, Joseph still honored God. Joseph did his best, whether he was in prison or in the king's palace. He never complained, and he never stopped following God. God blessed him and fulfilled his dreams, just as He promised.

Our game today is a lot like life sometimes. We don't always know where we're going, and we never know when someone might pull the chair out from under us! But we need to do our best to always follow God and honor Him no matter what. Just like with Joseph, God will see to it that the dreams we have that come from Him are fulfilled.

Have players say this chant as they slowly walk around the tight circle: "We can honor God when life's not fair. We can honor God, sitting in a chair." They should say the chant over and over while walking, until you say, "Sit!" At that point, they should each feel for a chair and sit in it. The player left standing without a chair sits in "jail," safely off to the side of the circle, out of the way of the blindfolded children. Remove one chair and continue play until only one player remains. For safety reasons, children should keep one hand on the shoulder of the child in front of them at all times, until they reach down for a chair. When down to two or three players, they keep their hands on the chair instead of each other's shoulders.

LINK it up

Joseph did nothing wrong, yet it seemed everything wrong happened to him. We can learn from Joseph that life is not always fair to us, but that God will never leave us. When we honor Him, He will honor us.

* **Think of a time you were treated unfairly. How did you respond? How could you have responded better?** *(Answers will vary. Be sure to share from your own life experience to encourage discussion.)*

* **What's a good way to honor God when someone treats us unfairly?** *(I can pray for that person, I should not always try to be right, etc.)*

* **In our game, you couldn't see where you were going or where the chairs were. If you don't know what to do in a situation, who are some good people to follow to give you direction?** *(God, my parents, my pastor, etc.)*

A Star Is Born

Teams follow the star and learn about Jesus' prophesied birth.

Bible Basis:

Isaiah 7:14; 9:1–7;
Micah 5:2

Memory Verse:

For to us a child is born, to us a son is given. Isaiah 9:6

BIBLE background

The Old Testament prophets, like Isaiah and Micah, were chosen by God to be the spiritual leaders of His people. God used prophets to guide His people, give them warnings, or offer them insight into future happenings. The prophecies that were given concerning Jesus were special revelations that offered God's people hope for the future.

God used these prophecies to remind the Israelites that He was still in charge and that He would send a Messiah, or anointed One, who would reign over all.

Because of the prophets' messages, the people who believed in God lived with a constant hope that God's promised Savior would come. At the time of Jesus' birth, no one was exactly sure what this Messiah would be like. Ideas ranged from seeing Him as a powerful military leader who would deliver Israel from Rome, to His being an earthly king, to His being a lowly servant.

In some ways, Jesus was all these things. But He was also so much more. Jesus was God's very own Son in the flesh. And even after seeing Him, many still did not believe. Looking back at the prophecies, we can see how God was preparing the world over hundreds of years for its King and Savior.

level:
Low to moderate

group size:
Small to medium,
enough for two teams

space required:
Classroom or gym

TEACHER tips

* Discuss "words of encouragement" and what helping others looks and sounds like. As play begins, immediately point out players who are doing a great job of this. This will help players focus on success and not frustrations.

* For added challenge, use fewer, but larger triangles. Two players will need to stand on one star. If players step on the floor in the playing area, they must return to the starting side of the playing area.

* To simplify, make large stars instead of triangles. Only one star per player, plus one extra star per team, is needed.

STUFF
you need

◎ Construction paper

◎ Scissors

◎ Masking tape

WARM up

1. Cut the largest equilateral triangles (triangles with 3 sides of equal lengths) possible from construction paper. You will need twice as many triangles as players, plus 2 extra.

2. Mark off a 6-foot by 20-foot playing area with masking tape or other boundary marker.

ACTion!

Old Testament prophets, like Isaiah and Micah, told about Jesus hundreds of years before He was born. Because it was such a long time until Jesus came, the prophets' words about Him were written down for people to read. In fact, one time Jesus read aloud the very words that Isaiah had said about Him!

God uses prophets to show people what lies ahead and to point them in the right direction. In our game, you will use triangles to form stars that will point you from the starting line to the finish line.

Have two teams line up single file, facing each other, on the shortest side of the playing area. Tape an X behind the last player on each team. Place a pile of triangles for each team on the Xs.

When I say, "Go!" the last person in line picks up one triangle and passes it forward until it reaches the first player. The first player places it on the floor in the playing area. The last person in line then picks up the next triangle and passes it forward. When the second triangle reaches the first player, it's placed on top of the first triangle, upside-down, forming a six-point star.

Once a star is formed, a player steps on it and advances toward the other side. Teams must work together passing triangles, forming stars, and advancing players—one at a time—across the playing area. When players reach the other side, play goes in reverse, and the last player picks up triangles—one at a time—as players move off the playing area onto the other side. Once the triangles reach the other side, they are placed on the X. The team to accomplish this first wins.

Players can only have one triangle at a time. Players must remain on a star at all times while in the playing area.

LINK it up

God promised us a Savior. He used Old Testament prophets to point people to their Savior. The prophets told people exactly where Jesus would be born and what He would be like while He was on earth.

* How does a star make us think of Jesus? *(Jesus brings light to the darkness, His birth was announced by a star, Jesus is a guide in the same way the North Star is a guide, etc.)*

* What were some of the things that were said about Jesus before He was born? *(He would be born in Bethlehem, He would rule over Israel, He would come as a baby, He would be born of a virgin, etc.)*

✱ Just as the stars in our game kept you walking in the right direction and moving forward, how can prophecies help you step closer to God? *(When we see how prophecies are fulfilled, we are encouraged about the truth of God's Word and the direction He leads us in our daily lives.)*

Infinity and Beyond

Dribbling balls through "infinity" helps players realize God's Word is forever.

Bible Basis:
Jeremiah 36;
Isaiah 40:8

Memory Verse:
Your word, O Lord, is eternal. Psalm 119:89

BIBLE background

Jeremiah was both a priest and a prophet who functioned as a spokesperson for God to His people, though the people refused to listen to him. Jeremiah was God's mouthpiece during the reign of the last five kings of Judah, proclaiming judgment, repentance, and God's restoration for those who obeyed. Some of the kings listened to God's words; some did not. One king who did not listen was Jehoiakim.

God told Jeremiah to write on a scroll the words he was about to give him regarding Judah, Israel, and other nations. Jeremiah called for Baruch, who wrote the words as Jeremiah dictated them. Then Jeremiah instructed Baruch to read the scroll at the temple before the people of Judah. Afterward, King Jehoiakim called for the scroll to be delivered to him. As the scroll was being read to the king, he cut off pieces of it and burned it. It was obvious he had no fear of God or His words.

God told Jeremiah to again write down the same words on a scroll. In addition, God gave Jeremiah a specific warning to pass along to the king in regard to his treatment of the scroll. God would not allow His words to ever be destroyed.

Throughout the centuries, Satan has diligently and desperately tried to eliminate God's Word. In some countries, preaching or even reading the Bible means putting your life in danger. Ultimately, Satan will never be successful at his attempts. God has declared His Word "stands forever" (Isaiah 40:8). Nothing can destroy it or its power.

TEACHER tips

✽ Assign the third-position spot on the team to the player who has a hard time waiting for a turn. The player will be able to see how to play in advance and won't have to wait long to get involved.

✽ To increase excitement of play, add more balls and players.

✽ Let players use their hands or a broom to roll balls instead of using their feet.

WARM up

1. Tape or mark a 10- to 15-foot figure 8 on the floor or ground.

2. Mark a starting line on each end of the figure 8.

STUFF you need

◎ Masking tape

◎ Balls (at least 2)

ACTion!

Jeremiah was one of God's prophets sent to tell people that God wanted them to repent of bad things they had done. One time, God told Jeremiah to write down on a scroll the words He was going to give Jeremiah for the people of Judah. Jeremiah had Baruch write down the words as Jeremiah said them. After Baruch read the scroll to the people, the king of Judah asked to see it. When he got it, the king cut it up and burned it because he did not fear God. But God would not let His words be destroyed. He had Jeremiah write down what He said again on another scroll.

The figure 8 on the playing area looks a lot like the sign for infinity. Infinity is something that goes on forever without end. God's Word is like infinity because it is eternal and will last forever.

Divide players into two teams, and have each line up behind a starting line. Give a ball to the first player in line. To begin, the first player on each team puts the ball on the design on the floor. Players use their feet to dribble the balls on the taped line. One team dribbles in a clockwise direction while the other team travels counterclockwise.

Once a player travels completely around the figure 8, returning to the starting line, the next player in line takes the ball and continues dribbling around the figure 8 again. The first team to get all their players around the figure 8 wins. If the ball rolls out of the figure 8, the player who was dribbling must retrieve it and return to the starting line.

LINK it up

Jeremiah was a prophet of God who had to deliver some serious messages to God's people. A lot of people, like the king of Judah, did not want to hear God's words and tried to destroy them. But God said that His Word will stand forever and will never be destroyed.

* What can you think of that will last forever? (*God, His kingdom, heaven, God's love for each of us, etc.*)

* What are some ways people try to get rid of God's Word today? (*many countries won't allow Bibles, people sometimes get in trouble for talking about God, etc.*)

✻ **Why is it important to us that God's Word will last forever?** *(We are encouraged to know that nothing can put a stop to God's promises and truth. No matter what tries to oppose or battle God's Word, He will win the battle and we are on the right side.)*

Come-Mitt-Mints

Players are reminded of their commitment to Jesus in this game of mitts and mints.

Bible Basis:
Matthew 3:13–17;
Luke 3:21–23a;
John 1:29–34

Memory Verse:
*Do your best to present yourself to God as one approved, a workman who does not need to be ashamed.
2 Timothy 2:15*

BIBLE background

John the Baptist fulfilled Old Testament prophecy recorded in Isaiah 40:3–5 every time he helped people prepare to receive the promised Savior. Except for Jesus, everyone John baptized was a sinner. Jesus chose to obey the outward sign of commitment in order to "fulfill all righteousness" (Matt. 3:15). Jesus' baptism served as an example to those who would follow Him.

Jesus had reached adulthood. It was time for Him to begin the mission for which He had been sent. By being baptized, Jesus indicated that He was committed to following through on God's plan. Jesus' baptism was an event of consecration and the ushering in of His ministry years.

John did not want to baptize Jesus at first because he did not feel worthy to do so. He believed that Jesus should instead baptize him. But Jesus, understanding the significance of His baptism, told John, "It is proper for us to do this" (Matt. 3:15).

Likewise, we do not always understand why God asks us to do the things He does. In fact, sometimes His instructions appear to make no sense at all. But like John, we need to simply obey and thereby demonstrate our commitment to Him and His plan for us.

level:
Moderate to active

group size:
Medium,
enough for two teams

space required:
Classroom or gym

TEACHER tips

* Demonstrate how to pick up mints with a mitt, clarifying that only one piece may be picked up at a time.

* For added challenge, give each team fewer mitts than there are players.

* For easier play, remove the tag element from the game. With this method of play, there is no need for streamers.

WARM up

1. Set up chairs at opposite ends of the playing area.

2. Set a basket or box on each chair.

3. Spread candy on the floor throughout the playing area.

STUFF you need

◎ Assortment of mitts—oven mitts, mittens, etc. (2 per player)

◎ Individually wrapped candy mints (2 or 3 bags)

◎ 2 baskets or boxes

◎ 2 chairs

◎ 2 different colors of streamers

ACTion!

Divide players into two teams, and assign each a streamer color. Each player should tie a streamer around his or her right upper arm for easy identification. Have teams line up at the opposite end of their team basket. Give each player two mitts.

John the Baptist's job was to prepare people for Jesus. He told people to get ready to receive their Savior. One thing he did was baptize people in water as a sign of their commitment to God. John was surprised when Jesus came to him to be baptized. He felt Jesus should be baptizing him instead. But Jesus knew it was important to get baptized to show His commitment to God's plan. Today, our game involves *mitts and mints* to help remind us to show our commitment—our "come-mitt-mint"—to Jesus.

When I say, "Go!" each team will run into the playing area and pick up one mint at a time with your mitts. Players then run to place the mint in their team basket. But watch out, because a player from the other team may tag you. If you get tagged, you must drop one mitt and the mint wherever you get tagged and stand still. You can't move again until one of your teammates hands your mitt back to you.

Players can only move with the mitts on their hand and can only pick up and deliver mints to their basket with the mitts. The team with the most mints in their basket at the end of the game wins.

LINK it up

Jesus showed His commitment to God's plan for His life by having John the Baptist baptize Him in water. Baptism is a sign that we have made a commitment to follow God.

✱ How committed were you to your teammates when they got tagged? Were you more interested in helping them or picking up mints? (*Answers will vary.*)

✱ What are some ways we can show our commitment to Jesus? (*go to church regularly, read my Bible, pray for others, tell others about Jesus, etc.*)

✱ What are some commitments you have made to others? Have you stuck with these commitments? (*Answers will reflect commitments typical of your group—perhaps agreeing to perform chores at home, take care of a pet, or complete schoolwork on time. It's not easy for children to fulfill all their commitments, so encourage them by sharing your own challenges and victories in this area.*)

On Your Knees

You're only safe in this wild game of tag when you're on your knees!

Bible Basis:

Matthew 6:5–13; 14:23; 18:20; Mark 1:35

Memory Verse:

Devote yourselves to prayer, being watchful and thankful.
Colossians 4:2

BIBLE background

In Jesus' model prayer—the Lord's Prayer—He does not just provide a set of words to memorize, but a pattern to follow as we present our own thanks and concerns to God. The prayer begins with adoration, moves on to confession and requests or petitions, then closes with worship. According to Jesus' example, our prayers may follow that same pattern.

Jesus demonstrated both individual prayer (Matt. 14:23) as well as group prayer (Matt. 18:19–20). He also taught that we should approach God as children (Matt. 11:25–26). He praised God for revealing Himself to "little children" instead of to the "wise and learned."

Perhaps the most important thing Jesus taught us about prayer was that we should do it often. We frequently find verses like Matthew 14:23, where Jesus "went up on a mountainside by himself to pray." He got away every chance He could to be alone with His Father in prayer. Jesus understood the absolute necessity of prayer—He knew He couldn't live without it.

How much more do we need a regular prayer life today, with all the trials and troubles that continually surround us? Let's learn all we can about prayer from Jesus: how to pray, how not to pray, and especially how often to pray.

TEACHER tips

✱ Introduce the concept of a prayer shawl, used by Jewish men in Bible times. Jesus would have used one of these shawls during the morning Jewish prayer services, during the Torah service, or on special holidays. The cloth has special knotted fringe attached to each of its four corners and must contain a thread of blue. It is worn across the shoulders and draped over the head during prayer. Students will be using paper towels to stand in for prayer shawls.

✱ If shawls do not stay put, have players tuck them under the necks of their shirts. Shawls do not need to be exposed. This hidden element also keeps players from knowing how many squares remain on the other players.

✱ For added challenge, play on an extra-large field and designate a lot of players to be It.

✱ For easier play, have only one person be It. This allows players to move at a much slower pace or even walk to the other side.

STUFF you need

◎ Roll of paper towels

◎ Masking tape or other tool to mark boundaries and lines

WARM up

Set up established boundaries for the play area, including a starting line and a finish line that players can stand on.

ACTion!

Jesus is our ultimate example when it comes to prayer. He taught us to pray with our hearts and not just to be seen by others. He even gave us a model prayer to follow when we pray. Jesus often went off by Himself, usually very early in the morning, to meet with His Father in prayer. Jesus knew how important it was to speak to His Father and to hear from Him.

The Bible says that God is our safe hiding place. Whenever we pray, we have found a safe spot, no matter what is going on around us. In our game, your safe spot will be on your knees—it's the only way you can escape being tagged.

Choose two to four players to be It. Have these players stand in the center of the playing area. Give other players long strips of paper towels (three to five sections each) to drape around their shoulders as a prayer shawl. Explain what a prayer shawl is.

All players stand on the starting line. The object is for players to cross the finish line. While they're running, the players in the center may tag them. Whoever gets tagged must return to the starting line. Players are safe and cannot be tagged, however, if they're on their knees. But while on their knees, they also cannot move forward and must remain in the same spot.

Once a player is tagged, a section of the prayer shawl must be removed and left at the starting line. The player who reaches the finish line first or with the most squares left on the prayer shawl wins.

LINK it up

We should follow Jesus' example when we pray: pray often, get away by ourselves to meet with God, and don't pray just to be seen or heard by others. Prayer keeps us safe and draws us closer to Jesus. We can pray anytime, anywhere.

* **Why are we safe when we're on our knees?** (we're safe from the devil, we're getting stronger in God, we're alone with Jesus, etc.)

* **What do you find hardest about prayer?** (making time to pray regularly, knowing what to say to God, staying awake if praying at bedtime, etc.)

* **Why do you think it's important to pray if God already knows what we need?** (Being in a close relationship with God means telling Him about our lives, everything from our fears to our needs to our praises. We can't know another person very well if we never talk to him or listen to him! It's the same way as we grow closer to God and follow the path He has provided for us.)

Rooftop Race

Players learn the value of teamwork as they carry balloons to safety.

Bible Basis:
Mark 2:1–12; Luke 5:17–26

Memory Verse:
You may know that the Son of Man has authority on earth to forgive sins. Matthew 9:6

BIBLE background

When Jesus forgave the paralytic man's sins, He wanted to prove His authority over both disease and sin. The Pharisees who were present considered this blasphemy, a crime punishable by death (Lev. 24:15–16). They were appalled that Jesus claimed to be God.

The crowds, however, had a different reaction. Jesus was hugely popular with the masses at this time. He had begun His healing ministry, and crowds were drawn to Him like a magnet. The house where Jesus was ministering was probably the typical one-room, one-story, mud-brick house, which held 50 people at most. This house's capacity was at standing-room only, as evidenced by the paralyzed man's friends having to lower him through the roof. The crowd was "amazed" by what Jesus said and did. Their amazement probably stemmed mostly from Jesus claiming His authority was from God. Jesus used the man's healing as a visible sign of His power over invisible things, such as sin.

We can't always see where God is working in our lives, but that doesn't mean He isn't. He can just as easily forgive sin as heal, as He can provide protection or anything else we need. Release your faith to Him, assured that He is working both inwardly and outwardly in your life every day.

level:

Moderate

group size:

Medium, enough for at least
two teams

space required:

Gym or outdoors

TEACHER tips

✱ If playing outdoors, add a small
amount of water to balloons to
keep them from blowing away. Do
not allow children to throw the
balloons with water.

✱ For added challenge, when you
shout, "Jesus forgives!" have
players standing at starting lines
switch lines with the other team.
The children with blankets will have to cross each other's pathway to get to
their new starting location.

✱ For easier play, have the entire team grab the edge of the blanket, then go to
the balloon pile and load up as many as possible onto the blanket before
heading back to the starting line.

STUFF you need

◎ Balloons
(10 per team)

◎ Blankets
(1 for each team)

◎ Masking tape

WARM up

1. Blow up balloons.

2. Tape or mark starting lines about 15 feet away from the balloon pile.

*ACT*ion!

Jesus was teaching in a house so crowded, people were standing everywhere—even in the yard—just to hear Him teach and watch His miraculous healings. Across town were four men who had a very sick friend. This friend could not walk, so they put him on a mat and carried him all the way to the house where Jesus was. They couldn't get in through windows or doors, but this didn't stop them. They knew if they could get to Jesus, their friend would be healed.

The only thing they could do was carry the man to the rooftop. Once on the roof, they cut a hole in it and lowered him down onto the floor, still on his mat. Jesus was so impressed with their faith, He healed the man's body and forgave his sins.

Pretend these blankets are the sick man's mat. Work together, just as the friends did, to carry balloons on them. Whichever team ends up with the most balloons wins.

Divide the group into two teams. Each team begins with its first four players grabbing the corners of their blanket. Players run to the balloon pile, place a balloon on their blanket, then return to the starting line. After laying the blanket down, the next four players pick up its corners, run to the balloons, then put one more on the blanket. Teams continue in this manner, picking up a balloon on each trip, until all the balloons are gone. With each trip, the balloons that have already been picked up are left in the blanket as it is carried back to the balloon pile for more balloons. The team with the most balloons on its blanket after all the balloons are gone wins.

In case of a tie, the team that finishes first wins. If a balloon falls off the blanket during play, a player from that team must return it to the pile. Once balloons are on blankets, players may not touch them.

LINK it up

The sick man's friends cared enough to bring him to Jesus for healing. And Jesus did heal the sick man. Jesus did more than that, though—more than anyone expected. He forgave the sick man's sins. Jesus used His healing power to show that He also has the power to forgive sins. When we ask Him to forgive our sins, He forgives. Ask Him to forgive your sins, and tell your friends about Jesus' power to forgive sins too.

✳ **What is power?** *(Let kids describe it in their own words. They may describe people in positions of authority, things such as cars or engines, or natural forces like tornadoes.)*

* **When the four friends brought the sick man to Jesus, how did Jesus show He had power over sin?** *(He forgave the man's sin and He healed the man's body.)*

* **How can knowing Jesus has the power to forgive sin help you when you do wrong?** *(It makes confessing sin easier, because we know He is able to forgive. It helps to know that when He says He forgives, our sins really are forgiven.)*

Christ Cross

Teams race to build replica crosses from paper cups.

Bible Basis:
Mark 11:27–33; 12:1–12; 15:24–39

Memory Verse:
God did not send his Son into the world to condemn the world, but to save the world through him.
John 3:17

BIBLE background

Jesus was brought to Golgotha, where the crucifixion victims were drugged by wine vinegar to dull their senses. Jesus refused the wine because of His determination to endure the suffering brought as He took on the sin of humanity. Jesus was stripped, had His hands and feet pierced, and endured the mockery of passersby, all in fulfillment of prophecy.

At the cross, the religious leaders continued to mock Him. They said, "He saved others . . . but he can't save himself!" (Mark 15:31). Jesus sacrificed Himself so that others might be saved. At the moment of His death, the veil in the Most Holy Place was torn in two, from top to bottom. The tearing of the temple curtain separating the Holy Place from the Most Holy Place indicated that people now have free and open access to God. If we take advantage of that access, Jesus' death and resurrection can deal with the sin we confess.

As a born-again believer, you can be assured of the forgiveness of your sin. The issue of worthiness, acceptance, and love has been dealt with once and for all on the cross. You are now worthy, accepted, and loved by God as His own.

level:
Moderate

group size:
Small to medium; can be
played in teams or as a small-
group challenge

space required:
Classroom or gym

TEACHER tips

✱ Be sure teams know they must
rebuild the cross the way it was in
their starting box. If neither team
remembers how, let them bring
their cups back, then demonstrate
in the starting box how to build it.
Have them try again.

✱ For added challenge, have teams
cross each other's paths to place
cups in the box. Everyone starts in the same place, but players will build
crosses in the box the other team first had theirs in. Be sure players are
careful as they run across the other team's path.

✱ For easier play, instead of running from one box to another, have the teams
sit. Hand them cups to build their cross in the box in front of them.

STUFF
you need

◎ Large paper or
plastic cups
(24 per team)

◎ Masking tape

WARM up

1. Set up the playing area by taping 2 large rectangular areas (3-feet by 5-feet)
for each team, about 10 feet apart.

2. Set up 24 cups in each starting box in the shape of a cross.

ACTion!

When Adam and Eve sinned in the Garden of Eden, disobeying God by eating from the Tree of the Knowledge of Good and Evil, they brought sin into the world for all of mankind. Because of God's holy nature, this sin impacted His relationship with everyone who would ever live on earth. God knew His plan must be completed to bring people back into relationship with Himself.

He knew He'd have to give His very best—His Son, Jesus Christ. It took Jesus, who was perfect and without sin, to pay for the sin the rest of us are born with. Jesus died a very painful death on the cross. It wasn't just physical pain, but emotional and spiritual pain as well. It was emotional because He took all of our sin, sadness, and grief upon Himself. And it was spiritual, because when He died, He was totally separated from His Father.

We owe our very lives to Jesus and to His work on the cross He died on. Without the cross, none of us would have any hope for an eternity spent with Him and a lifetime of His love. Let today's game remind you of the amazing thing Jesus did for us by giving His very life on the cross.

Each team starts by standing behind their team's cups, which have been formed into a cross. All players will grab one cup at a time and run to the other box, where they'll rebuild their cross in the exact same way. Players take turns running back to the starting box until they've retrieved all their cups. The team that successfully rebuilds their cross first wins.

LINK it up

Jesus suffered a great deal and paid a huge price for our sin by dying on the cross. But His death was the only way God could redeem man back to Himself and pay off the debt of sin that we owed.

* What does Jesus' death on the cross mean to you? *(Allow students to answer.)*

* According to the memory verse, John 3:17, why did God send Jesus? *(To save the world. You may need to explain that though Jesus came to save people in our world, not all are willing to be saved.)*

* How can we show Jesus how much we appreciate what He did for us? *(by making a decision to follow Him, by remembering to thank Him and praise Him for what He did, by telling others about His death, etc.)*

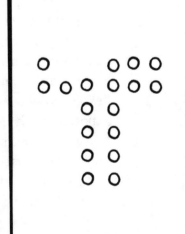

Good News Challenge

**Teams announce the good news
of Jesus' birth with newspaper shapes.**

Bible Basis:

Luke 2:1–20

Memory Verse:

*Today in the town of
David a Savior has been
born to you; he is Christ
the Lord. Luke 2:11*

BIBLE background

To comply with the Roman census, Joseph had to travel about 70 miles—at least a three-day journey—from Nazareth to Bethlehem, the home of his ancestor David. Mary was nearly ready to give birth, so it was not the best time for them to be traveling. Since they had no choice, God took care of them and in this way fulfilled a part of His plans.

Very few people would expect that the birth of the Savior would be announced to some lowly shepherds. In those days, shepherds were not thought of very highly, and even worse, most were considered to be thieves. But that's exactly to whom God chose to make His first announcement. When the angel appeared to them with God's good news, they were told they would find baby Jesus "wrapped in cloths and lying in a manger" (Luke 2:12). Most people would not have expected that either.

The King of the earth, God's own Son, was to be born in a stable and laid in a manger? That just doesn't sound possible. But God sometimes does things that, from a human perspective, seem out of the ordinary, and not always in a manner people expect. God showed the world from the very beginning of Jesus' life that although He would be their ruler, He would also be their servant. He would be able to relate to mankind in its humanity, even as He ultimately saved us from our humanity.

level:
Low to moderate

group size:
Any

space required:
Classroom or gym

TEACHER tips

✱ If one team struggles to work together, offer suggestions and demonstrate a better way to do the task.

✱ For added challenge, have a designated area where teams begin—away from the area where they'll create their shapes. Have teams run to a pile of newspaper and spread out the papers in a patchwork quilt to form the item that was called out. When the teams are finished, they'll run back to the starting area to shout, "Good news!" The team that finishes first wins.

✱ For easier play, have each team lay out nine pieces of newspaper in a large square on the floor. Have players use markers to draw the item that was called out. Be sure the drawing touches all nine pieces.

WARM up

On each index card, write a word from the Bible story that can be portrayed in a simple shape (tree, cross, manger, sheep, shepherd's hook, bell, angel, star, etc.). Sketch out the shape, in squares, on the card.

STUFF you need

◎ Index cards

◎ Markers

◎ Plenty of newspaper

ACTion!

God worked through the circumstances around Jesus' birth, including the trip to Bethlehem, the stable, and the manger or feed-box bed, to help people recognize Him.

He also chose to announce Jesus' birth to a few shepherds who were working in their fields. The shepherds knew where Jesus was born before just about anyone else. To make the grand announcement, God sent an angel to tell the good news to these shepherds. After the first angel delivered his message, a whole choir of angels appeared and sang praises to God. The shepherds were frightened by this, but they still left their field and went to find Jesus. Our game will remind us of the surroundings of Jesus' birth—a star, a sheep, and a manger.

Give each player a large foldout section of newspaper. Then divide players into teams. Draw a card from the pile, calling out the item listed. The players on each team then lay the newspaper on the floor, like a patchwork quilt, forming the shape of the item you called. Once the shape is formed, team members stand on their own piece of newspaper.

When they're satisfied with their creation, players shout, "Good news!" Award points for the first team to finish, the best teamwork, the most creative team, and so on. Then call out another item from the cards. Continue until all the shapes have been made. The team with the most points at the end of the game wins.

LINK it up

God chose to announce the good news of His Son's birth to some lowly shepherds who were in the field tending their sheep. They immediately obeyed the angels, who directed them to where Jesus was born, and they went to worship Him. Most people did not think their Savior would be laid in a manger.

* If you were one of the shepherds, how would you have reacted to the angels and their announcement? Scared? Surprised? Excited? Would you have believed what they told you? Why or why not? (*Allow students to answer.*)

* Why do you think God chose to have Jesus born in a stable with the animals? (*As students offer their answers, help them understand how God*

wanted His Son to be one of us—not a king on a throne, but a humble servant who would someday give His life for all of us.)

✱ **Jesus' birth came in a very unexpected way. Has God ever done anything in your life in an unexpected, surprising way?** *(Encourage your class members to see the unexpected in simple things as well as the big surprises of life. Be ready to share an example from your own life.)*

Family Circles

Hula hoop fun reminds players that God is into families!

Bible Basis:

Luke 2:39–40, 52;
Deuteronomy 6:6–9;
11:19; Matthew
13:54–56

Memory Verse:

Jesus grew in wisdom and stature, and in favor with God and men. Luke 2:52

BIBLE background

The Bible offers great detail concerning Jesus' lineage but doesn't tell much about His nuclear or extended family. What we know is pieced together from unrelated references. Matthew 13:55–56, for example, names James, Joseph, Simon, and Judas as Jesus' brothers, and also refers to an unspecified number of sisters. We also learn that Jesus' mother, Mary, was related to Elizabeth, John the Baptist's mother. Since the culture of that day included relationships among extended family, it's possible that Jesus grew up acquainted with John.

According to Luke 2:40, 52, Jesus was just like any other child in the way He had to grow up. He would have received formal instruction as well as informal teaching in the home. Twice a day He may have recited what we know to be Deuteronomy 6:4-5.

God has placed all of us in particular families for a reason. They are there to help us learn, grow, and experience God's perfect plan for our lives. We may not realize it at the time, but our families are God-ordained—intended by God Himself to give us the things we need.

TEACHER tips

✱ Large plastic hoops bend or break easily, especially if too many bodies are squeezed into them. Keep heavy tape handy for repairs if necessary. Optionally, thick nylon ropes made into loops the size of hoops may be used instead.

✱ For added challenge, make players keep hoops below their knees or above their heads as they return from the center circle. Or have all groups hop back on one foot.

✱ For easier play, instead of having groups return to the center circle, designate the winners as the group that gets the correct number of players in the hoop.

WARM up

1. Tape a circle 6- to 10-feet in diameter in the middle of the playing area.

2. Lay plastic hoops on the floor in the playing area as indicated on page 69. If using more than 4, spread them as far apart from each other as possible but equidistant from the center circle.

3. Make a game cube by taping shut all the sides of a small square box. Then, write the numbers 1 through 6 on the sides of the box in a random order (1 number per side).

STUFF you need

◎ Large plastic hoops about one yard or larger in diameter (at least 4)

◎ Game cube with numerals 1–6 written on sides. (As an option, instead of a game cube create a game spinner using a paper plate, brad, and paper clip.)

◎ Masking tape

ACTion!

God created families from the very beginning. Adam and Eve and their sons, Cain and Abel, became the first family. When Jesus was born, God put Him in a family too. He had brothers and sisters, and He had parents—Joseph and Mary. God wanted Jesus to grow up in a family so He could learn from them. He learned the teachings of the Jewish law, and He learned how to grow in many ways.

God has also created your family. He knew exactly which parents, grandparents, brothers, sisters, even aunts and uncles to give you! Your family may be unlike anyone else's, because He made every family unique and special. He has an awesome plan for each family to serve Him. We're going to work in "families" in our game today, trying to fit as many family members into hula hoops as possible.

The game begins with players standing in the center circle of the playing area. Roll the game cube. **When I say, "Welcome to the family circle of _____"** (fill in the blank with the number that was rolled), **everyone will run to the hoops. The number of players I called will step inside the hoop, pick it up, and run back to the center circle, with the hoop around the group of you. The first family back to the center of the playing area wins.**

Roll the game cube and begin play. If you roll a number one, all players run to the hoops. Players try to get as many inside the hoop as possible. The team that returns to the center circle with the most players wins that round.

Award team or individual points to winners. Play a specified number of rounds or until a designated number of points is reached.

LINK it up

When Jesus was born, God put Him in a family. God is all about families, and He made each one of them different. One way God cares and provides for us is through our families.

✳ In what ways was Jesus like any other child growing up? *(He had a family, He had to grow in wisdom and strength, He had to obey His parents, etc.)*

✳ Do you think Jesus knows what it's like for you in your family? Why? *(Answers will vary.)*

✳ What do you like best about being part of a family? What do you like least? *(Allow students to answer.)*

Jesus Heals Hurts

Players get all wrapped up in Jesus' heart for healing.

Bible Basis:
Luke 7:11–17

Memory Verse:
The Lord is full of compassion and mercy.
James 5:11

BIBLE background

The town of Nain was about 10 miles from Jesus' hometown of Nazareth, so it was probably familiar territory to Him. Luke 7:16–17 indicates that Jesus was well-accepted in Nain, even though He was rejected in His hometown (Matt. 13:54–58).

To be a widow in Jesus' day often meant absolute poverty. Having a son—who apparently was a grown man—was this widow's sole form of financial support. Jesus' heart of compassion rose up immediately when He saw this widow with her son, who was being carried off in a coffin. The only recorded words Jesus said to her before raising her son was, "Don't cry."

Jesus is the only one who can ultimately and effectively put an end to this world's suffering. He is able to heal physical, emotional, and spiritual pain. But now that He is no longer walking the earth raising people from the dead and comforting those who mourn, these works are done in the strength of the Holy Spirit. Jesus told us that those who believe in Him would do even greater works than He did (John 14:12). So don't hesitate to step out in faith in Jesus' power. A hurting world is waiting for us to show Jesus' compassion and mercy.

level:
Low

group size:
Small to medium, enough for
at least two teams

space required:
Classroom

TEACHER tips

✱ Be sure to balance the teams by
having players on both teams who
are skilled at writing.

✱ For added challenge, do not precut
the hearts. Give teams
construction paper, have them cut
out hearts, and write the hurts on
them. Place the paper for the
hearts about 20 feet from the
player being wrapped by the team. Team members will run to bring the
hearts one at a time to the player being wrapped. The team with the most
hearts wrapped up in their player at the end of the game wins.

✱ For easier play, have teams write or draw a heart and/or a hurt on each or on
every other square of bathroom tissue.

STUFF
you need

◎ Construction paper

◎ Scissors

◎ Rolls of bathroom
tissue (1 to 3 rolls
per team)

◎ Markers (washable,
1 per team)

WARM up

Cut construction paper into 3- to 4-inch hearts (12 hearts per team).

ACTion!

Distribute a marker, one to three rolls of tissue, and 12 hearts to each team.

When Jesus walked into the town of Nain with His disciples, He was met by a widow—a woman whose husband had died—who had now just lost her only son. This was obviously quite painful for the woman, and she was weeping when Jesus saw her. Jesus felt very bad about her sadness and told her not to cry anymore. Then he walked over to the son's coffin and told him to get up! The son did. He was alive once again!

Jesus has the power to heal all of our hurts. Sometimes we hurt in our body, and other times, like the widow, we hurt in our heart. Jesus doesn't want us to hurt at all. We can tell Him everywhere we hurt and trust that He will help us.

To start our game, each team needs to think of 12 kinds of hurts that people deal with and write them on your hearts. Then pick a teammate who wants to be wrapped in the tissue. As you wrap up your player, you must also wrap the hearts inside the layers of tissue. Just as you're wrapping up the hurts you wrote down, Jesus wraps our hurts and pains with His heart of compassion and love.

The team that wraps their player first with all 12 hearts is the winner. Optionally, the team that has the best or most creative hurts written on their hearts can be chosen as the winner.

LINK it up

Jesus hurts when we hurt. He is always willing and able to heal us of any hurts we may have. No hurt is too big or too small for Him to take care of. There is no need for us to hold on to any hurts when Jesus is ready to handle them for us.

* Of the hurts that you wrote on your hearts, which ones do you think are probably the hardest for people to deal with? Why? Would these be hard for Jesus to take care of? (Allow students to answer.)

* Have you had hurts that you've given to Jesus to heal? What happened? (As students share their answers, be prepared to tell about a hurt in your own life that you asked Jesus to heal.)

* Think of one person who you know is hurting—either physically or emotionally. Let's take a moment to pray for that person. (Allow children a moment to pray for others. Then lead them in a general prayer for Jesus to help those who are hurting.)

A Thankful Heart

This game helps players get "bowled" over with thankfulness toward God.

Bible Basis:

Luke 17:11–19

Memory Verse:

Enter his gates with thanksgiving and his courts with praise; give thanks to him and praise his name.
Psalm 100:4

BIBLE background

Bible-time leprosy caused lesions on the skin and the deterioration of muscles and nerves. Because it was highly contagious, lepers were forced to live outside the city and required to announce their uncleanness when anyone came near them. It was the priests' responsibility to determine if a person was leprous. The law required that people who believed their leprosy to be gone were to have their healing verified by a priest. When Jesus told the men to show themselves to the priests, He was telling them that their leprosy would be healed.

Just as Jesus promised, "as they went, they were cleansed" (Luke 17:14). Jesus did not lay hands on them to heal them. He did not command their healing to manifest as He did in many occasions. He simply told them to go to the priests. It must have taken great faith for these lepers to go to the priests without any prayer or touch from Jesus. But as they obeyed, they were cured—all of them.

Sadly, only one of the 10 came back to thank Jesus. While this obviously was a great miracle and very worthy of thanksgiving, what about all the often overlooked miracles that Jesus performs on our behalf every day: giving us strength to get out of bed each day, providing food for our tables, placing His beauty of nature all around us? It's easy to take all this for granted, but God wants us to be thankful in all things (1 Thess. 5:18).

level:
Low to moderate

group size:
Small to medium

space required:
Classroom

TEACHER tips

✱ Using permanent markers, have players write things they're thankful for on sides of milk jugs or plastic cups.

✱ For added challenge, when players get a ball that's been rolled, they should toss the ball to the other side of the circle, but not to the person who originally rolled the ball. The more balls in play, the more exciting and challenging.

✱ For easier play, have players sit around in a circle. One designated player will constantly feed balls to other players who must remain seated. The designated player may freely go in and out of the circle chasing balls and handing them to the players.

WARM up

1. Tape a large circle on the floor.

2. Cut out a heart and tape it to a milk jug.

3. Place all milk jugs within the circle area.

STUFF you need

◎ Empty milk jugs or large plastic cups

◎ Small foam or plastic balls (1 per player)

◎ 1 piece of construction paper

◎ Masking tape

◎ Markers

ACTion!

Give each player a ball, and have everyone spread out evenly around the circle. Place the jug or cup with the heart somewhere in the circle near the other jugs.

God wants us to be thankful people. He wants us to appreciate everything that He does for us, whether it's something big or something little. When Jesus healed the 10 lepers, only one of them came back to thank Jesus for his healing. Jesus asked that man why the others didn't come back. It's important to God that we have grateful and thankful hearts.

As we're playing our game today, think of things you're thankful for. Try to knock down as many jugs as you can, pretending that each jug stands for one thing you're thankful for. But don't knock down the jug with the heart on it. That jug stands for the one leper who came back to thank Jesus. Every time you knock down a jug, you'll get one point. If you knock down the leper's jug, you'll lose a point. The person with the most points at the end of the game wins. Keep track of your own points.

Players stay behind the circle line, taking turns rolling balls toward jugs. If the jug with the heart on it gets knocked over, the player who knocked it over must quickly run into the circle and set it back up. If players have to run into the circle to pick up a ball, they must do so quickly and set up any jugs they knock over. Players must always be behind the circle line before rolling balls. Game is over when a designated number of points or time limit has been reached.

LINK it up

Jesus healed 10 lepers, but only one came back to thank Him. Jesus asked the one who did come back what happened to the others. God notices when we do not have grateful hearts. Jesus is pleased when we thank Him.

✱ Why do you think the nine lepers didn't come back to thank Jesus for healing them? *(they didn't think it was important, they didn't want to take the time, they didn't have grateful hearts, etc.)*

✱ **How does it make you feel when you do something nice for someone and don't get thanked for it?** (*Answers will likely focus on feelings of being hurt, taken for granted, ignored, sad, etc.*)

✱ **How can we keep a thankful heart for all God does for us?** (*pay attention to His blessings, remember to thank Him and praise Him often, don't be a complainer, etc.*)

Heart Attack

Which heart will God's (flash) light reveal next?

Bible Basis:
Luke 18:9–14

Memory Verse:
I the Lord search the heart and examine the mind. Jeremiah 17:10

BIBLE background

The Pharisees were considered religious purists who were concerned with keeping the letter of the law. They did all they could to separate themselves from those they thought were unclean. A tax collector would certainly fall into that category. Tax collectors were the most despicable of all people, often considered traitors. Pharisees did not want tax collectors to be used as witnesses or given honorary offices.

Jesus zeroed in on the attitudes of the hearts of the two types of people in His parable. The lesson in the Bible story may be compared to the Lord's declaration to Samuel about David. The Lord looked at David's heart rather than his outward appearance (1 Sam. 16:7). Like David, the tax collector in today's story had a heart of humility toward God.

We need to be careful when we start getting confident in our own righteousness. We must remember that everything we have and everything we are is a gift from God. If it wasn't for the grace of Jesus, we wouldn't be righteous at all. It is always best to err on the side of humility and allow God to raise us up, rather than fall into self-righteousness and cause God to humble us (see Matt. 23:12).

level:
Low to moderate

group size:
Small

space required:
Classroom

TEACHER tips

* If playing on tile, use clear self-adhesive paper to keep hearts taped to the floor. Simply cut a square of the paper, place over the heart, and adhere to the tile. Clear, self-adhesive paper will come up easily. (Not recommended for carpets.)

* For added challenge, turn out the lights! Optionally, spread hearts farther apart. Increased distance makes the game more difficult. Additionally, penalize players if they touch the floor instead of landing on a heart by having them sit out for a period of time. Or have them start from a certain spot if they touch the floor.

* For easier play, players sit in a tight circle on the floor. Place a heart in front of each player. Use a flashlight to quickly light the different hearts. Players try to slap their hands on the heart before the light is removed from it.

WARM up

1. Cut construction paper into very large hearts (twice as many as the number of players).

2. Tape the paper hearts to the floor (randomly or in a pattern) within a large square playing area, about a foot apart.

3. Place a chair in one corner of the playing area.

STUFF you need

◎ Construction paper

◎ Scissors

◎ Masking tape

◎ Flashlight

◎ Chair

◎ Optional: clear, self-adhesive paper

ACTion!

Have players begin the game by standing on a heart. You should stand on the chair.

The Pharisees always thought they were better than anyone else, and they spent a great deal of time trying to prove it. The Pharisee in Jesus' parable thanked God that he was not like the tax collector—a sinner. But the truth was, the Pharisee was also a sinner because his heart was not right before God.

While it's good to do good things and behave properly, God is most concerned about the attitude of our hearts. If we act one way on the outside but are thinking another way on the inside, God will know it. He searches our hearts and knows if we are truly loving, caring, and humble people, or if we're just pretending.

Just like the flashlight we're going to use in our game, God's Word also shines light onto our hearts. It reveals hidden secrets and evil intents. There's no escaping the light of the Holy Spirit.

Start the game by shining the flashlight onto one of the hearts. All players try to get to that heart. They can only get to the heart by jumping onto another heart. They cannot jump onto a heart already occupied by another player, but they can jump out of the playing area, run around it, then jump back into it on a different heart.

As soon as a player reaches the lighted heart, shine the light on a different heart. Keep moving the light until you have finished playing.

LINK it up

If we're not careful, we can be just like the Pharisees. We might do things just so others will notice us, or we may wrongly make judgments about other people. But God sees our hearts, not just our actions. Jesus says that the attitude of our hearts is important.

* Why was the Pharisee a sinner, even though he thought he was less sinful than other people? *(His heart wasn't right with God, but he wasn't humble enough to see that.)*

* What is wrong with judging others by looking at their outside appearance, their actions, or anything else? *(We can be very wrong about other people. We might find out later that a person's heart is very different from what we thought we saw on the outside. God says we are not to judge others, according to Matthew 7:1–2 and Luke 6:37.)*

✱ **Do you think it's good or bad that God judges our hearts and not just our actions? Why?** *(Answers will vary. If a person's heart is right with God, his or her actions should reflect that. But sometimes people choose to act in a way that hides their real feelings and beliefs. God can see right through a person's efforts to appear good and knows the deepest truth about everyone's hearts.)*

Oh Say, Can You See?

A fun way to learn that the Holy Spirit helps us understand Scripture.

Bible Basis:
Luke 24:13–35

Memory Verse:
Whoever has my commands and obeys them, he is the one who loves me. John 14:21

BIBLE background

The two followers of Jesus who walked to Emmaus did not believe the women's story or that Jesus was the Messiah. Before the Resurrection, the disciples still thought their Messiah would be one to come and save them by overthrowing the evil Roman government. It's possible that when Jesus spoke in parables, the disciples thought He was strictly speaking metaphorically about His death and resurrection.

When Jesus spoke to them on the road to Emmaus, He explained what was said about Himself "beginning with Moses and all the Prophets" (Luke 24:27). Though the two men didn't recognize Jesus physically at first, they sensed His presence as He explained the Scriptures to them (Luke 24:32).

It's only through revelation knowledge given by the Holy Spirit that we are able to know Jesus at all. When Jesus asked Simon Peter who he thought He was, Simon answered, "the Son of the living God" (Matt. 16:16). Jesus told him he was blessed because that knowledge was revealed to him by God Himself (Matt. 16:17). The Holy Spirit opens our spiritual eyes so we may see Jesus through the Scriptures and sense His presence in our lives.

If you're having a hard time connecting with God or understanding His Word, ask that the "eyes of your heart may be enlightened" (Eph. 1:18) so you can see Him more clearly.

level:
Low to moderate

group size:
Small to medium

space required:
Classroom

TEACHER tips

✱ When setting up obstacle courses, be sure to set the objects a few feet apart. This will keep items from being so close together that they pose a tripping hazard or so far apart that they are difficult to find.

✱ For added safety, have a teammate walk closely next to the blindfolded players as a safety guide. They may not give instructions, but are to stop the blindfolded teammate from running into or tripping over objects.

✱ Ensure that the children do not run through the course while blindfolded.

✱ Remind kids that although speed is a goal, if they move too fast they won't be able to hear or respond to instructions well. They should move at a moderate speed. Also point out that tripping, running into objects, or needing help from the safety guide will slow them down. They may win by taking time.

STUFF you need

◎ Blindfolds (1 per team)

◎ Several chairs

◎ Tables

◎ Other objects to serve as obstacles

WARM up

1. Create basic blindfolds from strips of cloth.

2. Set up chairs, tables, and other objects into simple obstacle courses, one for each team of children.

ACTion!

Divide the group into two or more teams.

When Jesus met two travelers on the road to Emmaus, He spoke to them from the Scriptures about His death and resurrection, which was foretold by Old Testament prophets. The travelers didn't recognize Jesus, and He didn't reveal Himself right away. He wanted them to believe, by faith, that He was their Messiah who died and was now alive again.

It wasn't until Jesus ate dinner with them that night that the Holy Spirit opened their eyes to recognize Jesus. When we read God's Word, the Holy Spirit will open our eyes as well—not our natural eyes, but our spiritual eyes—so we can see Jesus and understand Scripture. Our game reminds us that Jesus helps us understand what the Scripture says, which tells us what God wants us to do.

We're going to go through an obstacle course. Sounds fun, doesn't it? Did I mention you'll have to do it blindfolded? Your teammates, using only their voices, will guide you through the course. Like the Holy Spirit helping us to understand Scripture, your teammates will help you get through the obstacle course. We'll see who listens carefully and who completes the course first.

Explain how the teams must move through the courses (around the chairs, under the tables, etc.). Be sure to watch at all times to ensure the blindfolded children stay safe. Play until everyone takes a turn completing the obstacle course.

LINK it up

Jesus opened up the Scriptures to the men on their way to Emmaus. Likewise, the Holy Spirit will open our eyes to see Jesus with our hearts and to help us understand His Word.

* Even though we can't physically see Jesus, have you ever sensed His presence like the travelers did? How? *(Answers will vary.)*

* Why would you want to understand God's Word? *(When we understand God's Word, we learn more about who God is, how He wants us to live, and the truth about the things that happen in the world.)*

* What are some ways you can get to know the Bible better? *(reading the Bible every day, memorizing verses, asking a parent to help find verses about a certain problem, etc.)*

Full Nets

Get as many fish as possible into the net. It's time to follow Jesus!

Bible Basis:
John 1:35–42;
Matthew 4:18–22;
Mark 3:13–19a

Memory Verse:
You are my friends if you do what I command.
John 15:14

BIBLE background

All four gospels record the story of Jesus calling His 12 disciples. The disciples came from different geographic regions, and all had different jobs. And, as we learn from the many Bible stories involving Jesus' disciples, they had quite an array of personalities!

Jesus called two brothers, Peter and Andrew, as they were casting their fishing net into the Sea of Galilee. When He saw them, He said, "Come, follow me . . . and I will make you fishers of men" (Matt. 4:19). As Matthew records it, the two immediately dropped their nets and followed Jesus.

When we give our hearts to God and make a commitment to follow Him, He doesn't ask for any prerequisites from us. All He wants is immediate obedience. Jesus wants all of us to be fishers of men, regardless of whether or not we feel we qualify. His calling is our qualification. He will equip and prepare us as we step out in obedience to do His work. So drop your net and go!

level:
Moderate

group size:
Enough for two teams

space required:
Classroom or gym

TEACHER tips

* Large party stores or craft stores typically carry fishnets. A large blanket, sheet, or shower curtain may also be used.

* For added challenge, every once in a while, empty the net by shouting, "Huge wave!" Explain that a huge wave emptied the net or perhaps a player rocked the boat and tipped it over, also emptying the net. Additionally, allow players to only use their feet to kick balloons into the net.

* For easier play, have players stand around the edges of the net, alternating players from each team. Players grab the edge of the net while balloons are thrown onto it. Have the group raise and lower the net to get other team's balloons off. The team with the most balloons still on the net at the end of the game wins.

WARM up

Inflate 12 colored balloons for each team. With a marker, write "1" on half of the balloons and "2" on the other half.

STUFF you need

◎ Large fishing net, blanket, sheet, or shower curtain

◎ Balloons—a different color for each team (12 per team)

◎ Permanent marker

ACTion!

Divide the players into two teams. Start with each team on opposite sides of the playing area, with balloons spread out inside the playing area. Be sure to mix up colors of balloons.

When Jesus began His ministry, He knew He'd need some help. He wanted to find people He could teach about God so that after He died, His work would continue. He decided to choose 12 men to be on His team. These 12 were from different places and all had different jobs. Jesus knew they were the ones God wanted Him to teach and work with.

As He called the disciples to come and follow Him, they immediately left whatever they were doing and ran after Him. They knew there was something special about Jesus, and they wanted to be with Him. A couple of the men He called were fishermen. They dropped their fishing nets and followed Jesus the very same day He called them.

The object of our game is to get as many fish—balloons for your team—as possible into the net. Play begins when a designated person runs through the playing area dragging the net across the floor. (As an alternative, two players can drag the net.) All players then enter the playing area and toss their balloons onto the moving net. Players may only pick up one balloon at a time and only balloons with their team number. Play stops when the person with the net runs out of the playing area. Decide ahead of time how much time the person will be in the playing area with the net. Give a signal when time is up. Whichever team has the most fish in the net after time is up wins.

LINK it up

The first disciples that Jesus called to follow Him came from very different walks of life. They were from different places, and they had different kinds of jobs. But no matter what his background was, when each one was called to be a disciple of Jesus, he immediately left the life he knew and followed Jesus to bring others to God. Jesus wants us to follow Him.

✻ **What do you think it would have been like to be one of Jesus' 12 disciples?** *(Allow students to answer.)*

✱ **Why is it so important to obey God immediately instead of waiting until a better time?** *(I show God that I love Him and want to put Him first, I let God know that I am committed to Him, etc.)*

✱ **How can you show God you are committed to following Him?**
(by obeying Him, by learning all I can about Him, by praying regularly, by serving Him, etc.)

All Is Well

Teams engage in a wet and wild race to overflow their wells.

Bible Basis:
John 4:3–43

Memory Verse:
The Father has sent his Son to be the Savior of the world. 1 John 4:14

BIBLE background

Jesus, who was Jewish, traveled through the land of Samaria instead of avoiding it like most Jews of His day would do. The Jews and Samaritans had hated each other for hundreds of years. Not only did Jesus purposely go into Samaria, He also stopped to talk to a woman. This also was unheard of, as women were considered second-class citizens, and men did not speak to them in public. But Jesus was known for breaking some customs now and then.

Jesus knew this woman's story before she told Him. He knew she was living an immoral life and was probably estranged from her community—possibly even her family. It was important for Jesus to talk to her, because He wanted her to know that her Messiah had come and that He could offer her a way out of her condemning lifestyle.

As soon as Jesus revealed Himself to her, she ran back to her town and told her story about meeting Jesus. Verse 39 reveals that "Many of the Samaritans from that town believed in [Jesus] because of the woman's testimony." Jesus reached out to one person, and a revival was sparked throughout her entire town! This can still happen today. All it takes is one person, set ablaze by God's Spirit, who is willing to reach out to another—possibly one shunned by others—and an entire city can be turned upside-down for Christ.

level:
Moderate

group size:
Enough for two teams

space required:
Gym or outdoors

TEACHER tips

* Since this game involves water play, which sometimes gets a little messy, place towels under the buckets and jugs to keep things less slippery.

* If a child is reluctant to play because of getting wet, offer a special job such as monitoring the wells to see how full they're getting. Don't force a child to play, and watch for those who may tease children who don't want to play.

* For added challenge, when the first player is at the beginning of the line for the second time with the cup, give the team two cups. Now two players from the same team can go simultaneously. If play continues long enough for the first player to have a third turn, add three cups to the team. Continue the pattern until one team wins.

* For easier play, instead of having each team member run, have teams form a long line from the water bucket to the milk jug. The player closest to the bucket begins the game by scooping a cup of water and passing it to the next player. Players keep passing the cup until it reaches the last player, who empties the cup into the jug. Players then pass the cup back down the line to fill it again. Once the cup returns to the bucket, give the team two cups to pass. Continue adding cups until a team wins.

WARM up

1. Set up playing area.

2. Place empty milk jugs at least 20 feet from the starting lines of each team.

3. Place a bucket of water at each starting line.

4. Place a cup in the bucket of water. (Have back-up cups ready in case one breaks.)

STUFF you need

◎ Plastic, gallon milk jug with small cap opening (1 per team)

◎ Plastic buckets filled with water (1 per team)

◎ Cups—paper or plastic (several per team)

ACTion!

Have teams line up at the starting lines. (Teams must have an equal number of players.)

A woman from Samaria came to get water from a well. When Jesus saw her, He asked her for a drink. He told her He could give her living water, which would keep her from ever thirsting again. The woman didn't understand all that Jesus was telling her, and she didn't know who He was. Then Jesus began telling her about her life, so she thought He must be a prophet. Finally, when Jesus had finished talking to her, He told her He was the Messiah she'd been waiting for.

The woman ran back to tell the people of her town that she had just met the Christ—the Messiah. They came to meet Jesus, and they believed for themselves that He was the long-awaited Savior.

According to the customs of the times, Jesus shouldn't have even spoken to this woman. Jewish people didn't like Samaritans, and men were not supposed to talk to women in public. For Jesus, though, helping the woman hear the good news of eternal life was more important than such customs.

Today's game reminds us of Jesus and the woman at the well. In Jesus' time, it was hard to draw water from wells and then carry it all the way back to the villages.

To begin, the first player on each team fills the cup at the well (the bucket) and then runs to the jug. The players dump the water into their team's jug and then return to the starting line, passing the cup to next player. Play continues until one team fills their jug to overflowing.

LINK it up

In Jesus' time, men did not speak to women in public, and Jewish people, like Jesus, did not associate with people of Samaria. But these customs didn't keep Jesus from reaching out to the woman at the well. Jesus wanted to make sure she heard the message that He offers eternal life to all people.

* Are you comfortable trying to make friends with people who are different from you? Why or why not? (Answers will vary.)

✱ **Jesus told the woman at the well that whoever drinks the water He offers would never thirst again. What does that mean to you?** *(Jesus' love and salvation fill us up on the inside, forever keeping us alive and refreshed.)*

✱ **When have you reached out to tell someone about Jesus? What happened?** *(As students are thinking of their answers, be prepared to share a story from your own life experience.)*

Lots of Leftovers

See how many leftovers can be gathered from Jesus' miracle feeding.

Bible Basis:

John 6:1–15

Memory Verse:

My God will meet all your needs according to his glorious riches in Christ Jesus.
Philippians 4:19

BIBLE background

The crowd that followed Jesus to the hillside by the Sea of Galilee had obviously been following Him for quite a while, as Jesus was concerned that they were probably hungry. The text indicates that there were five thousand men there that day, but this does not include women and children, who probably at least doubled that number.

Jesus asked Philip where they could go to buy food for the people, but He had no intention of grocery shopping. He was testing Philip to see where his faith was. Philip failed the test by telling Jesus that there was no way they could afford to feed all those people. Just then, Andrew alerted Jesus to a little boy who had five loaves of bread and two fish, although Andrew wasn't holding out much hope that the boy's two-piece fish dinner was going to help. It was a desperate situation. Too many people, too little food, and too little money.

Perfect time for a miracle! After Jesus instructed everyone to sit, He gave thanks for the food, then passed it around. The more He distributed, the more there was. The food multiplied before the crowd's eyes. Not only did everyone have enough to eat, but the disciples collected 12 baskets of leftovers!

What's your desperate situation? Family problems? Financial lack? Health concerns? Sounds like the perfect time for a miracle. Put it in Jesus' hands, and watch in amazement what He can do.

level:
Active

group size:
Enough for two teams

space required:
Classroom or gym

TEACHER tips

✱ Instead of colored cotton balls, use two different colors of wrapped candy or mini-marshmallows.

✱ For added challenge, consider incorporating additional elements to the game. Examples include: Players may only pick up a cotton ball if they are in a group of five (loaves) or two (fish), and the group must remain attached at all times. Or, teams must crawl, hop, or remain back-to-back with a partner, locked at the elbows, while in the playing area.

✱ For easier play, tape a circle on the floor, with baskets placed inside the circle. Teams toss cotton balls into the baskets instead of running throughout the playing area.

STUFF you need

◎ 2 bags of cotton balls—1 white, 1 another color

◎ 12 baskets or containers

WARM up

1. Set up a large playing area.

2. Spread out 12 baskets in playing area.

3. Spread out all of the cotton balls in the playing area.

*ACT*ion!

Have teams line up on opposite sides of the playing area. Designate one cotton ball color for each team.

Jesus was moved with compassion when He saw all the people who had followed Him to hear Him teach. He knew they must be very hungry. He asked His disciple, Philip, where they should go to buy food for the people, although He already had another plan in mind. A little boy had two pieces of fish and some bread and was willing to give it to Jesus. Andrew, another of Jesus' disciples, didn't think that the two-piece fish dinner was going to help all that much.

But Jesus doesn't need much to work with. He will take whatever we give Him and turn it into a lot when we have faith that He can. After Jesus passed around the food, it had multiplied so much the disciples had to pick up leftovers! When they finished, they had collected 12 baskets of leftover food.

We have 12 baskets in our game today that represent the baskets of leftovers. Each team is responsible for picking up leftovers (cotton balls) and putting them in the baskets. The team that collects the most leftovers wins the game. The only catch is that you won't know until the end which basket has been selected to determine the winner.

At your signal, all players run into the playing area. They are to each pick up one cotton ball at a time and put it in a basket, repeating to pick up as many individual cotton balls as they can. (If players do not abide by this one-at-a-time rule, empty one basket back into playing area.) After all cotton balls are picked up, players return to their side of the playing area. Secretly choose one basket. The team with the most cotton balls in that basket wins. Dump all the baskets and start again.

LINK it up

Jesus was concerned that the crowd that had followed Him to hear Him teach was getting very hungry. His compassion for them led to His miracle of multiplying a couple of pieces of fish and some bread into enough food to feed thousands of people!

✱ **What is a miracle?** *(When God uses His power to make something happen that could never happen otherwise.)* **Has God ever done a miracle in your life or in the life of someone you know? What happened?** *(Answers will vary.)*

✱ **Jesus met the needs of the people by feeding them. How does Jesus meet your needs?** *(He provides us with what we need, He puts people in our lives to help us with what we need, etc.)*

✱ **Do you think there's anything that's too hard for God? Explain your answer.** *(Allow students to answer.)*

Flock Together

Players learn the importance of unity as they flock with "birds of a feather."

Bible Basis:
Acts 1:12–14; 2:1–14, 21–24, 32–47; 1 Corinthians 16:19

Memory Verse:
They devoted themselves to the apostles' teaching and to the fellowship, to the breaking of bread and to prayer. Acts 2:42

BIBLE background

Pentecost was a strategic time for God to send His Holy Spirit to the disciples. During the festival of Pentecost in Jerusalem, there were "God-fearing Jews from every nation under heaven" (Acts 2:5). Those who traveled to the festival would return to their homelands—and take the message of salvation with them. They would be integral in spreading the gospel around the world.

After Pentecost, believers continued to meet regularly together. Not only did they meet at the temple "every day" (Acts 2:46), but they met in each other's homes and ate together. They grew in unity, and "the Lord added to their number daily those who were being saved" (Acts 2:47).

God is just as concerned with unity among His people today as He was during the birthing of the early church. When we are not unified and in agreement as children of God, we cannot succeed in building His kingdom (Luke 11:17). God does not want His church divided over issues of doctrine and segregated by race or nationality. There is power in unity!

We are also encouraged to meet together regularly (Heb.10:25). Likely, this instruction refers to more than just a weekly church gathering. It's important for Christians to fellowship together to strengthen, encourage, and comfort one another. If you haven't already, find fellow believers to regularly meet, pray, and discuss God's Word with. You'll be glad you did.

TEACHER tips

✱ Catch players doing the right thing. Whenever a player is being helpful or saying kind words, point it out. Draw attention to the skills, attitudes, and words the players should be using.

✱ For added challenge, once groups gather together, have an entire group do an action with their feathers, such as having all players balance a feather on their nose or on one knee or keep it in the air by blowing it.

✱ For easier play, have players sit around the small circle as a group, and give each player a feather. Have children pass feathers around the circle. When you shout, "Stop!" have players hold onto the feather they have. They then find feathers to match the color they have. The group with the most feathers wins.

✱ If allergies to feathers are a concern, try cutting feathers out of construction paper or using colorful silk leaves instead.

WARM up

1. Mark playing area with tape, forming a 3-foot circle.

2. Tape a 10- to 15-foot circle around the smaller one.

3. Place all feathers inside the smaller circle.

STUFF you need

◎ 1 package of multicolored feathers

◎ Masking tape

ACTion!

Have all players stand on the outside circle.

During the festival of Pentecost held in Jerusalem, God told early believers to gather together in a room and wait for His Holy Spirit. When His Holy Spirit came in the form of a "violent wind" and "tongues of fire," everyone in that room was able to speak in other languages. The people who had traveled to Jerusalem for the festival heard this, and it became a sign and wonder to them.

After Pentecost, the early church began meeting together regularly, both at the temple and in each other's homes. They stayed unified by thinking and believing the same thing. Because of this, God worked many miracles through them. God wants us to be in agreement with each other as His followers. There's power to do His work when we think and act in unity. He does not want us fighting with each other, because that grieves the Spirit and drains power.

Just as the early church gathered, or flocked together, we're going to be doing the same thing in our game. When I say, "Birds of a feather," everyone runs into the middle circle and grabs a feather. Then return to the outer circle. I'll then say, "Flock together." Now you must find other players with the same color feather as you. All players with the same feather colors must flock together.

Once groups are gathered, have them repeat together the memory verse.

LINK it up

When the early church met together at Pentecost, God sent His Holy Spirit, and miraculous things happened. The church continued to meet together regularly—in the temple and in people's homes. They had such unity among them that many people were saved, and the disciples were able to perform amazing deeds thanks to the power of God. We gather together today because we believe in Jesus.

✱ Why was it important for the early church to be in unity, with everyone getting along and believing the same way? (it helped the believers to grow stronger in their faith, it set an example for others outside the church, it brought people together to support one another, etc.)

✱ **Do you think it's still important today for God's people to be in unity and agreement? Why or why not?** *(Answers will vary.)*

✱ **Why is it necessary for Christians to meet together regularly?** *(to learn about God together, to help each other, to get to know other Christians, etc.)*

All Scrolls Lead to Jesus

Teams try to stay on the Bible pathway as they learn about the Bible's role in our lives.

Bible Basis:

Romans 1:1–17; 15:1–6, 23–24; 1 Corinthians 15:1–4; Galatians 1:11–12; Ephesians 4:20–32

Memory Verse:

Everything that was written in the past was written to teach us.
Romans 15:4

BIBLE background

The Bible is not simply an old history book with interesting stories. Nor is it a book that was relevant for society at one time but no longer matters to our lives today. Every book in the Bible, whether Old or New Testament, has paths that lead us straight to Jesus and His eternal plan of redemption for all mankind. That is something that transcends the ages and will never go out of style.

Paul, who wrote nearly two-thirds of the New Testament, met the risen Jesus in a very dramatic encounter on his way to Damascus. He spent the rest of his life planting and developing churches wherever he traveled. The New Testament is mostly comprised of his letters of encouragement, correction, and guidance to these churches. It's from these letters that believers receive great insight into how we are to live the Christian life. The same truths that he wrote about thousands of years ago are still quite relevant for us today.

The Old Testament, with its rich lessons in character studies of God's heroes of faith, can also provide us with much useful information as to what God expects of His people and how to stay on His path of blessing. It points forward to the fulfillment of God's prophecies for a Messiah.

The Bible is our roadmap into eternity, filled with guideposts to keep us heading in the right direction every step of the way.

TEACHER tips

❋ Garbage bags packaged in
continuous rolls are more durable
than paper towels and will not
separate as easily.

❋ For added challenge, provide more
roadblocks for teams, or add your
own roadblocks. While placing a
roadblock in front of a team, say, "You let your friend guide you rather than
the Bible; you took a wrong turn."

❋ For easier play, don't provide
any roadblocks.

WARM up

1. Have 2 teams line up 20 feet
apart.

2. Each team needs 2 long
sections of paper towels of
equal length. The entire
team must be able to stand
on the length.

STUFF you need

◎ Rolls of paper
towels (2 per team)

◎ Beanbags or flying
disks (3 per team)

◎ Masking tape

ACTion!

Divide your group into two teams, with each team standing behind its team line and facing the other team. Give each team two "scrolls" of paper towels and three beanbags or flying disks.

Many people believe the Bible is outdated and not important for us today. But the Bible is for all ages and for all people. Every book in the Bible, whether Old or New Testament, points to Jesus and to the gospel message of having eternal life through Him.

The Bible teaches us how to have a close relationship with the Creator of the universe. By following Scripture, we can avoid trouble and receive God's blessing on our lives. The Bible has an answer for every problem or situation we may encounter and helps us learn to be like Jesus.

We'll be using scrolls in our game. The Bible was originally written on scrolls, or rolled-up paper. The object of the game is to be the first team to reach the other team's line by using your scrolls as a pathway. Remember, the Bible guides us today!

Have teams roll out their first scroll behind their team line, facing the other team. To begin the game, teams roll out the second scroll in the playing area, then have all team members stand on it, advancing toward the other side. Teams then roll up their first scroll and unroll it in front of the second, which advances them closer to the opposite team line.

Scrolls must be rolled up when being picked up and passed. A team can block the other team's pathway by tossing a beanbag or disk within one foot of the front of the team's scroll. That team cannot place the next scroll forward; team members must place it sideways or parallel to the line they're trying to reach. Teams only have three chances to block the other team.

The first team to the other side wins. If a player falls off the path, the entire team must start again at the original starting line.

LINK it up

The Bible is just as important to us today as it ever has been. God does not change over time, and He still wants us to rely on His Word to guide us and help us make the right decisions. When we follow the Bible, we can be sure to stay on the right path!

* **How can the Bible guide us in our everyday lives?** *(it can show me right from wrong, it can help me grow closer to God by knowing Him better, it can help me make the right choices, etc.)*

✱ **Why do you think some people don't believe the Bible is useful today?**
(Allow students to answer. Point out that some people think they know everything about running their lives without other instruction or guidance, and others find it hard to believe in things they can't see or feel physically.)

✱ **Why is it important to memorize verses from the Bible?** *(having God's Word in our minds helps us to follow it when most needed; we may not always have a Bible handy, but when we have the truth in our hearts, we can call on it at any time and in any place; etc.)*

Serving Others Workout

Serving one another is fun with these crazy exercises.

Bible Basis:
3 John 1–14

Memory Verse:
Always give yourselves fully to the work of the Lord.
1 Corinthians 15:58

BIBLE background

During the time when John wrote this letter to Gaius, it was common practice for believers in the church to welcome missionaries into their homes when they traveled. They would then send the missionaries off again with provisions for the road. Early believers considered such hospitality a way for them to serve the Lord and co-labor with the missionaries in spreading the Gospel.

In his letter, John was praising Gaius for his faithfulness to take care of the missionaries who came to him, even though they were strangers. Gaius obviously had a servant's heart and wanted to do what he could to help God's people. News of Gaius's hospitality spread, and John heard about it when the missionaries "told the church about [his] love" (3 John 6).

No act of kindness that we show to others, especially to those laboring for the sake of the Gospel, will go unnoticed by God. And when we maintain a servant's heart—a heart of humility—He will allow others to take notice as well. Make it a point to show hospitality or kindness to a church staff member or a missionary you know. If you can't do something personally for that person, perhaps you could send a care package or write a note of encouragement to him or her. The person serving God will be blessed by your kindness, and you will be honored by God.

level:
Moderate to active

group size:
Any

space required:
Classroom, gym,
or outdoors

TEACHER tips

✱ After each pair has been to two or three stations, change partners by having children stand in a circle so that one group of teams forms an inside circle while the other pairs make an outside circle. Have one of the groups move around the circle until you tell them to stop. The players facing each other now form a new pair.

✱ For added challenge, have two sets of partners at each station. Each pair competes with the other.

✱ For easier play, after explaining the stations, allow pairs to wander to any stations they choose. Do not put time constraints on activities.

WARM up

1. Set up 6 workout stations by marking each plate with the station number and title.

2. Set up items listed at each station:

Station #1—Leap Frog: Use tape to mark a start and finish line 15 feet apart.

Station #2—Row, Row, Row Your Boat: Place 2 to 4 balloons in this area.

Station #3—Wheelbarrow: Mark start and finish lines at 15 feet or less. Place chairs at even intervals between lines for players to weave around.

Station #4—Lift Off: Place 2 to 4 balloons in this area.

Station #5—Three-Legged Challenge: Place socks or scarves in this area. Mark start and finish lines. Place chairs at even intervals between lines.

Station #6—Bouncing Ball: Place 2 to 4 balls in this area.

STUFF you need

◎ 6 paper plates
◎ Marker
◎ 6 to 12 balloons
◎ 2 to 4 long socks or scarves
◎ 2 to 4 balls
◎ 8 cones or chairs
◎ Masking tape

*ACT*ion!

Before starting, have all players sit as a group.

John wrote a letter to Gaius, praising him for being faithful to the missionaries he had taken care of. Apparently Gaius welcomed them into his home as they traveled around preaching about Jesus. Gaius had a servant's heart and wanted to help God's people. God likes it when we serve others, because when we do, we are really serving Him.

We're going to serve each other today as we play our game. Each of the workout stations involves an activity that must be done with a partner. You and your partner will need to serve each other in order to complete the activity.

Explain each of the following stations, and ask for volunteers to demonstrate activities.

Station #1—Leap Frog: Partners take turns scrunching down, then hopping over each other. They'll go from starting line to finish line and back again. (Teaches how to overcome obstacles together.)

Station #2—Row, Row, Row Your Boat: Partners sit on the floor facing each other with legs apart (in a V-shape) and feet touching. They'll pass balloons to each other using only their elbows. (Teaches how to share the workload.)

Station #3—Wheelbarrow: One partner puts hands on the floor while the other holds up the partner's legs. They'll start at one end and weave between the cones or chairs, then switch places for the return trip. (Teaches how to help carry another's load.)

Station #4—Lift Off: Partners stand back-to-back, locking elbows. They take turns launching a balloon in the air with their feet, trying to pass it back and forth. (Teaches how to lift each other's spirits.)

Station #5—Three-Legged Challenge: Partners each tie one of their legs to the other partner's leg at the ankles using a sock or scarf. Together, they weave around the cones or chairs. (Teaches how to lean on each other.)

Station #6—Bouncing Ball: Partners bounce a ball between them. As one partner bounces the ball, the receiving partner must twirl around once before catching it. (Teaches how to have a ball together.)

Explain how to rotate stations by going in sequential order. Pair up partners and place them at the different stations. Designate a certain amount of time to spend at each station; then have partners move to the next station.

LINK it up

Gaius was a servant of God who showed hospitality to missionaries traveling through his town. The missionaries told the church about the love and care Gaius showed them. It's a big deal to God when we show kindness to others and serve them with God's love.

✱ How is serving others the same as serving God? *(Answers will vary.)*

✱ In what ways do you like to serve others? In what areas are you good at serving? *(Allow students to share. Be ready to include your own story.)*

✱ What are some ways we can serve missionaries who work to spread the gospel around the world? *(we can send them care packages when they are away from home, we can write them letters, we can support them in prayer, etc.)*

Rock the Room Games SCRIPTURE AND TOPIC INDEX

The following index allows you to use this book with any curriculum.
Simply find the Scripture your lesson is based on or the topic you are teaching.

Scripture	Topic	Page
Genesis 1:6–13, 28–29	Creation	6
Genesis 1:26—2:25; 3:8	Creation	10
Genesis 4:1–16	Honesty, Sin	14
Genesis 8:1—9:17	God's promise	18
Genesis 13	Getting along with others	22
Genesis 22:1–19	Trust	26
Genesis 27:41—33:17	Forgiveness	30
Genesis 39:1—41:57	Faithfulness	34
Deuteronomy 6:6–9; 11:19	Family	66
Isaiah 7:14; 9:1–7	God's promise	38
Isaiah 40:8	God's Word	42
Jeremiah 36	God's Word	42
Micah 5:2	God's promise	38
Matthew 3:13–17	Commitment	46
Matthew 4:18–22	Disciples, Evangelism	86
Matthew 6:5–13; 14:23; 18:20	Prayer	50
Matthew 13:54–56	Family	66
Mark 1:35	Prayer	50
Mark 2:1–12	Forgiveness, Healing	54
Mark 3:13–19a	Disciples, Evangelism	86
Mark 11:27–33; 12:1–12; 15:24–39	The cross	58
Luke 2:1–20	Jesus' birth	62
Luke 2:39–40, 52	Family	66
Luke 3:21–23a	Commitment	46
Luke 5:17–26	Forgiveness, Healing	54
Luke 7:11–17	Compassion, Healing	70
Luke 17:11–19	Healing, Thankfulness	74
Luke 18:9–14	Judging	78
Luke 24:13–35	God's Word	82
John 1:29–34	Commitment	46
John 1:35–42	Disciples, Evangelism	86
John 4:3–43	Evangelism, Sin	90
John 6:1–15	Jesus provides	94
Acts 1:12–14; 2:1–14, 21–24, 32–47	Church, Disciples, Evangelism, Unity	98
Romans 1:1–17; 15:1–6, 23–24	God's Word	102
1 Corinthians 15:1–4	God's Word	102
1 Corinthians 16:19	Church, Disciples, Evangelism, Unity	98
Galatians 1:11–12	God's Word	102
Ephesians 4:20–32	God's Word	102
3 John 1–14	Serving	106

Rock the Room Games CORRELATION CHART

Each activity correlates to a Unit and Lesson in the curriculum lines shown below.
For further help on how to use the chart see page 5.

Title	Page	Scripture Reference	David C. Cook BIL LifeLINKS to God College Press Reformation Press Wesley Anglican	Echoes The Cross
Creation Scramble	6	Genesis 1:6–13, 28–29	Unit 1, Lesson 2	Unit 1, Lesson 2
Body Building	10	Genesis 1:26—2:25; 3:8	Unit 1, Lesson 4	Unit 1, Lesson 4
Stomping Out Sin	14	Genesis 4:1–16	Unit 2, Lesson 6	Unit 2, Lesson 6
Rainbow Rescue	18	Genesis 8:1—9:17	Unit 2, Lesson 8	Unit 2, Lesson 8
Get-Along Land	22	Genesis 13	Unit 3, Lesson 10	Unit 3, Lesson 10
Tic-Tac-Totally Trust God	26	Genesis 22:1–19	Unit 3, Lesson 12	
A Star Is Born	38	Isaiah 7:14; 9:1–7; Micah 5:2	Unit 4, Lesson 1	
Good News Challenge	62	Luke 2:1–20	Unit 4, Lesson 3	Unit 4, Lesson 3
Family Circles	66	Luke 2:39–40, 52 Matthew 13:54–56; Deuteronomy 6:6–9;	Unit 5, Lesson 5	Unit 5, Lesson 5
Come-Mitt-Mints	46	Matthew 3:13–17; Luke 3:21–23a; John 1:29–34	Unit 5, Lesson 7	Unit 5, Lesson 8
Full Nets	86	John 1:35–42; Matthew 4:18–22; Mark 3:13–19a	Unit 5, Lesson 9	
Jesus Heals Hurts	70	Luke 7:11–17	Unit 6, Lesson 11	
Lots of Leftovers	94	John 6:1–15	Unit 6, Lesson 13	Unit 6, Lesson 12
Rooftop Race	54	Mark 2:1–12; Luke 5:17–26	Unit 7, Lesson 2	
Christ Cross	58	Mark 11:27–33; 12:1–12; 15:24–39	Unit 7, Lesson 4	
Oh Say, Can You See?	82	Luke 24:13–35	Unit 8, Lesson 6	
All Is Well	90	John 4:3–43	Unit 8, Lesson 8	Unit 7, Lesson 2
Race to Forgive	30	Genesis 27:41—33:17	Unit 9, Lesson 10	Unit 9, Lesson 10
Unfair Chair Game	34	Genesis 39:1—41:57	Unit 9, Lesson 12	Unit 9, Lesson 12
Flock Together	98	Acts 1:12–14; 2:1–14, 21–24, 32–47; 1 Corinthians 16:19	Unit 10, Lesson 1	
Serving Others Workout	106	3 John 1–14	Unit 10, Lesson 3	
On Your Knees	50	Matthew 6:5–13; 14:23; 18:20; Mark 1:35	Unit 11, Lesson 5	Unit 11, Lesson 5
Heart Attack	78	Luke 18:9–14	Unit 11, Lesson 7	Unit 11, Lesson 8
A Thankful Heart	74	Luke 17:11–19	Unit 11, Lesson 9	Unit 11, Lesson 9
Infinity and Beyond	42	Jeremiah 36; Isaiah 40:8	Unit 12, Lesson 11	Unit 12, Lesson 11
All Scrolls Lead to Jesus	102	Romans 1:1–17; 15:1–6, 23–24; 1 Corinthians 15:1–4; Galatians 1:11–12; Ephesians 4:20–32	Unit 12, Lesson 13	